HOW TO LIVE WITH A MENTALLY ILL PERSON

Other Books by Christine Adamec

There ARE Babies to Adopt
Start and Run a Profitable Freelance Writing Business
When Your Pet Dies

HOW TO LIVE WITH A MENTALLY ILL PERSON

A Handbook of Day-to-Day Strategies

Christine Adamec

Foreword by
D. J. Jaffe, Board Member
National Alliance for the Mentally Ill (NAMI)

John Wiley & Sons, Inc.

New York • Chichester • Brisbane • Toronto • Singapore

Library of Congress Cataloging-in-Publication Data:

Adamec, Christine A.
How to live with a mentally ill person / Christine Adamec.
p.   cm.
Includes bibliographical references and index.
ISBN 0-471-11420-0 (cloth : alk. paper). — ISBN 0-471-11419-7 (pbk. : alk. paper)
1. Mentally ill—Home care.   2. Mentally ill—Family relationships.   3. Caregivers.   4. Mentally ill—Care.   I. Title.
RC439.5.S33   1996
362.2—dc20   95-42076

I am dedicating this book to my beautiful daughter Jane, who has suffered the dark torments of schizophrenia and who has miraculously come back into the light— hopefully, to stay.

CONTENTS

PART FOUR

APPENDIXES

Contents

ACKNOWLEDGMENTS

Many people have assisted me in researching and writing this book. My husband John has given me encouragement, advice, and great doses of moral support.

D. J. Jaffe, a tireless and profoundly effective New York mental health activist and board member of the National Alliance for the Mentally Ill, has provided a wealth of information: names of people to interview, how-to information on critical issues, and much more. This book would not be what it is without him and I appreciate him very much.

I am also extremely grateful to the librarians who provided me with so much assistance. Thanks to the library staff at the DeGroodt Library in Palm Bay, Florida, particularly the following people: Megan McDonald, head of reference, Marie Faure, reference librarian, and Pam Hobson, reference assistant. In addition, Shirley Welch, inter-library loan librarian at the Central Brevard Library and Reference Center in Cocoa, Florida, worked very hard to locate the books and journal articles I needed, including some very obscure sources. I appreciate them all.

Thanks also goes to my editor, PJ Dempsey, who believed in the concept for this book and who has given me valuable critical comments that greatly enhanced the content.

I would also like to thank the many mental health professionals and other experts who provided me with thoughtful commentary and practical information: Samuel Jan Brakel, J.D., a law professor at DePaul University College of Law in Chicago and vice president of Administration, Legal Affairs and Program Development at the Isaac Ray Center; Laurie Flynn, executive director of the National Alliance for the Mentally Ill (NAMI) in Arlington, Virginia; Nancy J. Herman, Ph.D., a sociologist and researcher at the Central Michigan University in Mount Pleasant, Michigan; Richard Keefe, Ph.D., author and assistant professor of psychiatry at the Mount Sinai School of Medicine in New York City, New York; Marge Lenane, licensed clinical social worker (LCSW) and project coordinator of the Childhood Onset of Schizophrenia project at the National Institute for

Mental Health in Bethesda, Maryland; Neil Lombardi, M.D., a pediatric neurologist and vice president of medical services for St. Mary's Hospital for Children in Bayside, New York; Gary Mosher, M.D., a psychiatrist with Circles of Care in Merritt Island, Florida; David Sudderth, M.D., a neurologist with The Neurology Center in Naples, Florida; Bertram Warren, M.D., a psychiatrist in private practice in Fanwood, New Jersey, who is also clinical director of the Union County Psychiatric Clinic in Plainfield, New Jersey, and the former president of the New Jersey Psychiatric Association; and Peter Weiden, M.D., director of the schizophrenia program at St. Lukes–Roosevelt Hospital Center in New York City.

I'd also like to thank the many interviewees who shared their personal stories with me. Holly Cmiel, a Florida mother of adult twins who are mentally ill, was a great help to me, as were the numerous others who needed to maintain their privacy but gave me candid information and opinions about their experiences.

FOREWORD

It's a pervasive and painful problem, although most people don't think about it until it happens to someone in their family, as caregivers throughout the United States and the world will attest. Yet it's a traumatic problem that happens in the best of families. It's called "mental illness," and it involves serious neurobiological disorders. And much of the time, it is the family that provides care and needs help coping with hallucinations, paranoia, and many other problems they may never have imagined. This book was written for these families.

Millions of people with neurobiological disorders live with their families. Sometimes it works and sometimes it doesn't. But either way, it's a constant struggle for caregivers of all ages.

How to Live with a Mentally Ill Person is a book for caregivers to people with serious illnesses such as schizophrenia, major depression, manic (bipolar) depression, and other neurobiological disorders (NBDs)—brain diseases that affect thinking and behavior. When your relative develops an NBD, you'll often find that your insurance is inadequate, the system is nonexistent or nonresponsive—and, if your relative is hospitalized, he or she is returned to you sicker and quicker. If your relative is poor, non-white, or a substance abuser, or is under age 18, multiply these problems. Clearly, families of people with NBDs need help.

An ongoing downsizing has also created a critical shortage of psychiatric beds in most areas, complicating problems for families. John Talbott, former president of the American Psychiatric Association, put it this way: "As a result of deinstitutionalization, families have become the doctors, the nurses, and the social workers. But if the family has become the replacement for the ward staff, it is a staff without shifts, without backup, without ability to enforce daily routines or medication compliance, without techniques or rehabilitation or the ability to access records."

These problems can be worked through if you understand the systems involved. *How to Live with a Mentally Ill Person* is a road map to help you comprehend and make your way through the morass of government and private organizations and your own personal turmoils as you struggle with your relative's illness.

Coping will be difficult—for the patient and for the family. Don't confuse the illness with the individual; instead, hate the disease but love the person. You will need to learn how to help someone who resists medicines or who exhibits psychotic behavior or threatens suicide. (Each year, about 15,000 people with mood disorders and 3,000 people with schizophrenia kill themselves.) *How to Live with a Mentally Ill Person* provides real examples of coping with real problems.

People with NBDs are not always able to control their own thoughts or moods. They may have visual, aural, or other hallucinations during periods when they are psychotic. They may exhibit "inappropriate" behavior and emotions such as laughing at the wrong time or at nothing, becoming excited for no discernible reason, or shrinking from people whom they perceive are persecuting them. Caregivers need tactics to cope with such behaviors. This book will help you.

Brain disorders are not curable. They are, however, controllable with medications. Modern medicines have come a long way in controlling symptoms and there is no shame in taking medicine to control the imbalance, just as there is no shame in taking medicine to control high blood pressure or diabetes. Unfortunately, finding the right medicine and the right dose can be a long, involved, trial-and-error process.

You will need to work with your relative's psychiatrist to learn what specific medications are supposed to do and what side effects may occur. And you will also want to ensure that doctor knows what effects this medication has on your relative. To do this, you need a good working relationship with a competent doctor, and this book will enable you to achieve this goal, as you learn how to find a good doctor, when to change doctors, and how to interact with the physician.

You also need to understand treatment settings, government hierarchies, entitlements, simple estate planning, and other issues you probably are not familiar with. They are critically important issues that mental health professionals rarely explain to families. They are covered in this book.

The author of *How to Live with a Mentally Ill Person*, Christine Adamec, is the parent of a young woman with an NBD and she personally understands the struggles that families go through in coping with the brain disease of a beloved family member. Unlike other authors who speculate endlessly on the "why" of NBDs, she accepts that they exist and instead concentrates on providing practical advice on dealing with the problems generated by your relative's NBD. This extremely helpful and practical book will arm you with the ability to cope effectively with the doctors, the bureaucrats, your friends and family, and your own very real fears.

D. J. JAFFE
New York, New York

D. J. Jaffe is a board member of the National Alliance for the Mentally Ill in Arlington, Virginia, and of Friends and Advocates of the Mentally Ill in New York City. Jaffe has been active for over seven years in educating families and trying to change the system to make it more responsive to those most in need. He travels the United States giving speeches on these issues.

INTRODUCTION

I know the pain, guilt, fear, and many other emotions that accompany being a caregiver to a mentally ill person, and I can truly empathize with my readers. In fact, one thing that had stuck in my mind since my adolescent daughter's first hospitalization, when she was age twelve, was a nurse saying to me, "Since you're a writer, maybe someday you can make some sense of all this and help others."

What a ridiculous statement that seemed to me at the time. I have never known such emotional pain as I felt then. It was literally the worst thing that had ever happened to me. Even though it wasn't directly happening to me, I was affected by Jane's illness, as were her father and her two brothers. I experienced the shame and the guilt, wondering and agonizing over what I could have done to make this child so sick. Wouldn't I know what it was, if it was that bad?

And now, five years later, I have come full circle and realize that I didn't do anything bad, nor did anyone else within my family or outside of it. Most mental illness is directly related to a brain dysfunction, not a dysfunctional family. That means the problem is not external—it is internal to the ill person.

How to Live with a Mentally Ill Person is for the many families who love their relatives and do their utmost to provide loving and good care—often at great emotional and financial cost to themselves.

One of the worst problems caregivers face is the overall stigma surrounding mental illness. This stigma causes caregivers, ashamed and alone, to hide their problems and suffer in silence. The emergence of such groups as the National Alliance for the Mentally Ill (NAMI) and its state member groups, as well as the increasing successes of pharmacological treatment, have eased this pain. Yet, sadly, the discriminatory mindset is still prevalent, and caregivers are still blamed by mental health professionals, the public, and themselves for a problem over which they have little control and did not cause.

If you are ashamed and despondent over your relative's condition and if you really don't know how to cope with such common problems as refusal to take medication, paranoid behavior, and other behaviors, how can you be an effective caregiver? The answer is that you can't. I want you to educate yourself and to be effective, and I want you to demand the utmost from your relative's physicians and other mental health professionals. This book is not only a discussion of the problem of providing care to a mentally ill person—with suggestions on how to resolve these problems—but it is also a rallying cry to stand up and assert your rights with the professionals who continue to blame and/or ignore you as you seek help for your relative.

The good news is that although families don't cause the problem, many families can help improve the situation, with information and understanding. There is information that caregivers need about common feelings and practical coping strategies. This is what I want to share with you. This is what I lacked when I needed it. I am writing the book that would have helped me when the crisis of mental illness engulfed my daughter and, through her, my family.

My goal in writing *How to Live with a Mentally Ill Person* is to provide you with practical information, tips, and strategies for optimizing your relationship with the ill person. Of course, I can't give you the magic answers that will make your relative well or even necessarily compliant. How I wish I could! But there is no one game plan or series of tactics that will work in every situation. However, what you can do, as you read through this book, is learn what others have felt and how others have managed. It is my hope that some of their strategies and tactics in effectively living with a mentally ill person will also work for you.

My research for this book included interviews with social workers, psychiatrists, and other mental health professionals. I also interviewed family caregivers, some of whom have resolved most of the problems of dealing with daily living with a mentally ill person and some of whom are still struggling to cope. My research also included searching databases on CompuServe and America Online, large computerized online services through which I found sources in medical, psychiatric, and popular literature. Special interest groups and libraries also provided valuable information; for example, I found the library files in the NAMI section of America Online very useful.

There are several "givens" in this book, underlying premises that I wish to explain up front. First, I believe that major mental illnesses, with few exceptions (such as the extremely rare multiple personality disorder), are biologically based diseases. Something in the brain goes awry and causes the person to experience the neurobiological illness, whether the disease is schizophrenia, depression, or some other serious psychiatric ailment.

I am not a psychiatrist, psychologist, or mental health professional, but I believe the expert researchers in this field who state unequivocally that mental illnesses are biologically based. Those people who don't think there is enough proof to support the neurobiological basis for mental illness bemuse me. They have essentially no proof that families or other people cause individuals to become mentally ill. Their old theories are based on more old theories and teachings that existed and proliferated before we knew much about the brain.

But I do want to stress that *How to Live with a Mentally Ill Person* is not a book that will teach you about the inner workings of the brain or why things may go wrong with it. Nor will I tell you how to "cure" such illnesses. In many cases, the mental illness you are contending with in your relative is a chronic problem with peaks and valleys. Medications may improve the condition but they will not cure the illness. Keep in mind that medications may improve symptoms or even the overall condition of the person. But remove the medication and the problem will recur.

I start from the premise that mental illness is biologically based and believe that families need plenty of help in adjusting to their ill relative's problems and coping with day-to-day life. As a result, my book deals with the family's response to the ill person and tactics and strategies to improve daily life with that person. For those who find that living with a mentally ill person is simply too much, I discuss letting go and finding a new place for your relative.

ATTRIBUTION

Each person who has been quoted by name in this book has signed a release authorizing the use of his or her name. In many cases, individuals did wish to be interviewed but did not want their identities revealed. Generally, this was because they were family caregivers providing very personal information about themselves and their family members, including how they felt about the circumstances they faced.

HOW THIS BOOK CAN HELP YOU

If you think you are the only person who has ever despaired of caring for a mentally ill person; the only person who has ever felt unable to bear another minute; the only person who has ever wondered why this terribly unfair thing has happened to you—this book is for you. While this book can't make the problem go away, it can provide advice from the experts—people who have faced this problem and the psychiatrists and others who truly empathize and offer practical advice to make it easier for you.

I want families to be empowered to use the knowledge that we have attained to date. Whether you have a child with manic depression or a spouse with major depression or a parent with Alzheimer's, I believe you share a common bond. This problem happened not only to the ill person, but to *you*. And you are not alone.

Millions of Americans suffer from disabling mental illnesses unrelated to alcohol and drug abuse, according to information provided by the National Institute of Mental Health. Most have living parents, many have brothers and sisters, and some are married. At least three to four million live with their families.

Although you might be willing to talk to your friends and relatives about a broad array of health problems, mental illness is often a subject you don't discuss. It's embarrassing, it's confusing, and it hurts too much, especially at first. We need to work on changing that.

How do you cope with caring for your ill relative, meeting your own needs, and dealing with a public that sees mentally ill people as fearsome or bad? This book includes suggestions and strategies for day-to-day living with a mentally ill person, as well as managing a life of your own and dealing with a biased population.

Not that we can change the world as well as ourselves in a week or a year or even in our lifetimes. But we can take steps, day by day. That is what I want you to do. Keep taking steps forward, even if they are "baby" steps. I believe the secret of success in virtually any venture, including difficult life circumstances, is to set goals and move toward them, even when it seems as if you are crawling. Every movement forward is an advance. And if you feel that you are "falling back," pick yourself up and move forward again. Do it for your ill relative and do it for yourself.

As I wrote this book, describing problems caregivers face and solutions and tactics, I kept saying to myself, "Be practical." As a result, whenever possible, I not only suggest *what* you might try but also *how* to try it. My overarching goal is to enable you to identify goals for yourself and your relative and to offer you ideas on how to move toward the goals that are right for you. I want to reduce despair and hopelessness and empower you as much as possible. Then when you are energized and empowered, you can spread the word to others.

HOW TO USE THIS BOOK

How to Live with a Mentally Ill Person is divided into chapters and separated into three major parts. The first part of the book covers how you and your family are initially affected by the mental illness of your relative and how you learn to accept it. The second part discusses problems and practical aspects of coping with living with your mentally ill relative. The third part covers working with the "systems"—the psychiatric hospital system, the educational system, and the insurance system (including Medicaid, Social Security disability, and Medicare). To a limited extent, I discuss the criminal justice and substance abuse systems, although that could be a book in itself—as could any of these other topics. Finally, in the Appendixes, I have included helpful books, organizations, and resources.

I recommend that you read this entire book. Each chapter contains information that may be of use to you in your current situation.

For example, information on coping with an elderly relative with dementia may include strategies that could be transferable for another caregiver who has a child with schizophrenia or a brother suffering from major depression. It is also true that some strategies that might work well with one individual would fail miserably with someone else. For example, gently touching or even bear-hugging a depressed person might work well, but a paranoid person might shrink back in terror. You need to tailor what you try with the person to his or her illness, the situation, and the individual's personality.

And sometimes, no matter how hard you try, no matter what you do, nothing seems to work. You might lose your temper and yell at the person or you might start crying and then worry what effect this will have on the mentally ill individual. It's important to remember that everyone "loses it" once in a while. Maybe this means you need some time off or maybe you need some rest. You also need information on how caregiving for a mentally ill person may affect you. This book will give you that information.

There are many books that discuss the diagnosis, treatment, and problems of various mental illnesses, as well as possible causes. This book is different. I will not attempt to tell you why mental illness occurs, although I do believe that there is a biological basis. Whether these illnesses are genetic, prenatally determined, or caused by some mysterious virus is well beyond the scope of my knowledge and abilities. So you won't read anything about "neuroreceptors" or other confusing medical terms here.

My goal is to talk about the difficulties that you as a caregiver face in living day to day with a mentally ill person. Knowing that many others have faced these problems is, in itself, heartening, because so many caregivers feel so terribly alone. I believe that knowledge is power and it's good to shed light on the everyday realities of living with a mentally ill person and how to make the experience more positive. I hope that you will find some useful and practical information and that it will help you to know that you are being guided by someone who has been there.

What is mental illness? For the purposes of this book, mental illness includes such serious and debilitating ailments as schizophrenia, manic depression (also known as bipolar disorder), major depression, panic disorder, schizoaffective disorder, anxiety attacks, obsessive–compulsive disorder and other debilitating neurobiological disorders, as well as combinations of them. These are generally severe long-term illnesses, often amenable to some form of treatment but not curable. Also, in some cases, such problems as attention deficit disorder can be very disabling to the individual and to the family, particularly when combined with other psychiatric problems. I include information for caregivers of people who have Alzheimer's or dementia because they face many of the same problems as caregivers to much younger mentally ill people.

If you're a caregiver to an adult or child with cancer, heart disease, leukemia, or other serious illnesses, many people consider you a hero. But if your relative is mentally ill, you are a suspect. And yet families are the mainstay for the majority of mentally ill people of all ages today. These caregivers need much more support and advice than they have received in the past from the mental health community.

How much do you owe your mentally ill child, spouse, sibling, adult child, or other relative? How much can you give? And if you completely sacrifice yourself to the care of the mentally ill person, do you understand that you may also be sacrificing the mentally healthy members of your family? These are tough questions with no "right" answers, but they are questions that families need to ask themselves and somehow resolve with a practical and hopeful plan, not by falling into an unconscious pattern of behavior. It is important to consider whether providing primary caregiving for the person is really in the mentally ill person's best interest.

I hope this book will help you resolve these issues in your life.

PART ONE

YOU AND YOUR FAMILY

This section is dedicated to discussions of how your relative's illness directly affects you and your family, including common emotional reactions many caregivers evince. My own personal story is included in this section. Maybe yours will be similar and maybe it will be very different, but you will probably find that you felt many of the same emotions and fears that I—and others—experienced. Whether you are a parent, spouse, or child of the ill person, this section should help.

You may think you're alone, but you're not. Beginning to accept the illness and trying to avoid subjugating all your own needs to the ill person are important aspects of effective coping, both of which are covered in this section. In addition, you will need both professional help and help from a good support group. How to find both is covered in this section.

1

THE IMPORTANCE OF THE CAREGIVER

Caregivers to chronically mentally ill people are very important. We care for people who would, in many cases, otherwise be homeless and completely dependent on handouts from shelters, soup kitchens, and welfare programs—or even worse. It is difficult and challenging to provide care for our relatives but we do it because we love them.

There are already plenty of homeless people in our communities. It is estimated that two-thirds of all homeless people are suffering from a serious mental illness. Without us, there would be far greater numbers of distraught and distressed individuals roaming the streets, or in jail. We caregivers try to make sure our relatives take their medication. We try to help them find a job, make friends, and live at least some semblance of a normal life. We provide around-the-clock love and care, and we do it for free.

And how does society respond to our efforts? With blame, derision, and shunning. Some of us hang our heads because we feel somehow at fault, even though we know we really didn't do anything to make the ill person sick. Some of us continue to wonder what terrible thing we did to cause such a problem—surely we would know what it was. The answer: We didn't cause it.

I know all of these feelings because I have had them, as the parent of a mentally ill adolescent. Now I think it is well past time to throw off our unseen chains, deal with our ill relatives as effectively as we can, and be proud of the job we're doing. It isn't easy, but I hope this book will help you learn coping strategies, understand that you're not alone, and give you some pride and self-confidence.

CAREGIVING TODAY

In earlier times, the institution was the primary provider of care for severely mentally ill people. But since the 1960s that situation has changed radically, and today it is the family that is the mainstay of the person with a neurobiological disorder (NBD). A neurobiological disorder is a chemical imbalance in the brain, such as schizophrenia, manic depression, major depression, Tourette's syndrome, panic disorder, anxiety disorder, and other severe mental illnesses, or combinations of severe mental illnesses.

The problems that caregivers of people with NBD face today are complex and profound. These problems arise from inside the family as well as from outside systems caregivers must deal with to help their relatives—educational systems, the hospital and medical systems, the criminal justice system, the insurance system and managed care, the work environment, and much more. It can be mentally and physically exhausting to traverse the bureaucratic mazes of each system.

This book is about what it's like to recognize and accept the fact that your family member has a mental illness; to learn to live with it and deal effectively with varying problems; and to avoid the error of completely sacrificing your own life out of a misguided sense of duty, martyrdom, or perceived necessity.

There are always choices, although we may not always like them. My goal is to help you recognize that there are choices, to find the choices available for you and your family, and to determine which is the best course of action for you. In some cases, you may not be able to continue to care for your mentally ill family member. It may be better if you don't, as hard as that can be to accept. If your mother, who suffers from Alzheimer's, constantly criticizes your children, if she exhausts you with her continual and increasing needs, or if she wanders off at night, you may need to consider another alternative. It is also true that the child, parent, spouse, or other relative may do better outside the home where you are not doing everything.

I've included in this book the key areas where your relative is likely to be affected and to affect others. You need to become your mentally ill relative's "case manager." This book will help you to do this.

Why the General Term "Mental Illness"?

I have not concentrated on one specific mental illness in this book, because whether you provide care for a person with schizophrenia, manic depression, obsessive-compulsive disorder, or some other illness, the family's responses are usually the same: shock, disbelief, denial, and so forth. (These reactions are covered in Chapter 2.) Coping mechanisms are also very similar.

Problems that you will experience as a caregiver also transcend specific diagnoses; for example, many people with neurobiological disorders are "noncompliant" when it comes to medication—they don't take it. Symptoms also may cross over diagnoses—paranoid behavior may be found in manic depression, psychotic depression, schizophrenia, or dementia in the elderly, to name a few.

In addition, no matter what disorder you are dealing with, you may find yourself frightened, burned-out, and worried about the future. These are only a few of the issues covered in this book. You may have to juggle the demands of work and caregiving, help your relative find and keep a job, and deal with many other problems that are commonly faced by caregivers.

LOOKING BACK IN HISTORY

How did we as a society get to where we are now? Let's take a brief look at the last two centuries of societal coping with mental illness.

The Eighteenth and Nineteenth Centuries

Williamsburg, Virginia, was the site of the first asylum for mentally ill people in the United States, which opened in 1769. There were few facilities for mentally ill people at the time and large numbers who were not in the care of their families were homeless or in prison, (as is the situation now).

A movement began in the 1830s and 1840s to construct institutions for the helpless and the homeless: poor people, mentally ill people, and orphans. Numerous asylums and almshouses were built, and by 1860, 28 out of the 33 states that existed at the time had asylums for psychotic people. In addition, people who were mentally ill and whose families could not care for them were frequently housed in almshouses ("poorhouses") along with orphans, poor people, and sometimes juvenile delinquents and criminals. Social reformers of the day considered this to be the answer. The ill people were fed and clothed, not left abandoned to wander about and fare for themselves. But disease and abuses were rampant, and the residents of almshouses were generally sick and miserably unhappy people.

By the late 1800s, social reformers decided that housing and care should continue to be provided for dependent populations, but severely mentally ill people would live in hospitals formerly called "asylums," and dependent children would live in orphanages—except for "defective" children. "Defective" at that time referred to mentally ill, developmentally delayed, or epileptic children (or, in the jargon of the time, insane, feeble-minded, and epileptic) who were often retained in the almshouse until the institution fell out of favor at the turn of the century.

The Twentieth Century

Moving ahead to the 1950s, many severely mentally ill people resided in state hospitals throughout the country. In 1955, there were about 559,000 psychiatric patients in state hospitals.

Families were not encouraged to have their ill members live with them or even to visit. In fact, relatives of the ill were actively discouraged from contact. The prevailing view in the first half of the twentieth century was that mentally ill people were very fragile and could not stand the stress and strain of a normal life with a family. The families were not blamed for the person's mental illness, but it was believed that the ill person should live away from home in a quiet and nonstimulating environment. If a relative did visit and the patient became excited, it was considered very bad by physicians of the time.

A New Presumption: Families Made Relatives Sick

In 1949, an influential study by psychoanalyst Trude Tietze was published in *Psychiatry* ("A Study of Mothers of Schizophrenic

Patients"). Tietze blamed the mothers of people with schizophrenia for the illness, stating that they were "domineering," and their children had a "warped psychosexual development." No longer was it bad luck, divine disfavor, or some other misfortune causing the illness: it was the primary caregiver—the mother. Dr. Anna Freud also believed the family was the problem.

This view spread rapidly and was accepted and adopted by psychoanalysts, the dominant therapists of the time. It was also adopted into the dominant societal thought. State or private hospitals were still perceived to be the best place for a mentally ill person to live. Certainly, it was presumed, ill people should not live at home, since it was believed that the mother had caused the psychosis in the first place. The family unit itself was also viewed as pathological. The negative view toward mothers and families as somehow causing mental illness continued through the 1960s and 1970s, and many people still accept this view today.

But in the early 1960s, a new social experiment began that was to drastically affect both people who were mentally ill and their families, as well as society at large. State hospitals had begun releasing mental patients into the community on a relatively small scale. But things heated up.

Deinstitutionalization

This planned social change occurred in 1963 with the passage of the Community Mental Health Act, which would lead to the closing or downsizing of many state hospitals. The plan was that mentally ill people were to be housed in the community. They would live with other like sufferers, not with their "bad" families, and be supervised by house parents or other individuals. Another impetus to deinstitutionalization was the development of psychiatric medications in the 1950s. It was presumed that ill persons outside institutions could be given medication or could take it themselves. But there were never enough places for mentally ill people to live, never enough community homes, and never enough people to supervise existing homes. So the exodus from the state hospitals resulted in many severely mentally ill people returning to their families.

Families at the time continued to accept that they must have done something terribly wrong to have caused their relative's illness. The psychiatrists and psychologists also persisted in this view. And still, mentally ill people were only briefly housed and treated in psychiatric hospitals, after which at least half of the institutionalized mentally ill people went back to live with their families.

The National Alliance for the Mentally Ill (NAMI)

This situation—families providing love and care and being berated by mental health professionals—could not continue. The creation of the National Alliance for the Mentally Ill in 1979 was the true beginning of the liberation of the caregiving family. Armed with new knowledge and theories and increasing evidence that mental illness was not caused by bad families but instead by genetics, physical illness, and other factors, these families stood together and declared that they were *not* going to accept the blame and derision anymore.

Their refusal to accept blame where credit was due had a burgeoning and strong effect on families nationwide and worldwide as mental health professionals rethought their position about the bad family and researchers intensified their efforts to find the actual causes for mental illnesses. In addition, new medications released many mentally ill people from their mental hells and proved that a biological agent can work against a brain disease, even when the ill person resides with the family.

But even as families began to receive a modicum of recognition for their often herculean efforts, other factors combined to exacerbate the problem and make the issue of dealing with the mentally ill tougher than ever.

KEY ISSUES AFFECTING THE MENTALLY ILL AND THEIR FAMILIES

Psychiatrists Say No to Mental Illness

Compounding the problem of deinstitutionalization, many psychiatrists and psychologists are reluctant to treat chronically mentally ill people out in the community. Instead, they prefer to treat neurotic people, the "worried well," who have temporary distressing problems. So there is a shortage of competent psychiatrists for seriously mentally ill people.

Why don't most mental health professionals want to treat seriously ill people? Wouldn't it be more rewarding to help a seriously mentally ill person than it would be to, for example, counsel someone who is unhappy with her job? Apparently not. People with severe mental illnesses are hard to treat and refractory. Doctors are frustrated when they do not see progress over years of treatment, or when they see improvement and then suddenly the person crashes back into psychosis, often for no discernible reason. Doctors like to see patients get better. Improvements in mentally ill people may be slight.

In addition, some psychiatrists deny the existence of mental illness altogether, believing that people who behave abnormally have merely chosen another way to live, as a sort of counter-cultural group. (This view, promoted by Drs. Laing and Szasz, proliferated widely in the 1960s and 1970s.) They believe that labeling people as mentally ill and treating them as mentally ill causes people to behave in the expected manner—psychotic. This view has been discredited.

Another related view was that psychiatric hospitals made people mentally ill. The reasoning was that if a sane person were placed in a mental hospital, the isolation, the rigid structure, and the overall atmosphere would make that person insane. That is why, they believed, people in state hospitals were mentally ill. Let them out and they would recover. This view persisted for years, although it was erroneous. Patients didn't recover when they left hospitals because these patients were truly sick *before* they had entered the state hospital. Merely being set "free" to navigate the complicated outside world, after years of the structured environment of the state hospital, was baffling and frightening to many former patients.

Advocacy and Patients' Rights

Another problem that has made life more difficult for both the mentally ill and their caregivers—as well as society at large—has been legal or private "advocates," whose mission is to press the issue of the rights of the mentally ill. In the worst case, they have pressured legislators to give mental patients the "right" to refuse hospitalization and treatment and to freeze and starve in the dark. It has been said that such people "die with their rights on." When Mayor Koch was in office in New York City, on one freezing January night he ordered the police to remove the homeless people from the streets and take them to shelters. Koch was instantly and roundly denounced by civil rights lawyers who sprung into action to keep the people on the dark, cold streets if they "wanted" to be there.

Over the past twenty years, attorneys who have become interested in the rights of the mentally ill, initially as an exciting new topic to explore, have managed to radically change the laws on mental illness, particularly regarding how and when an ill person could be hospitalized or treated against his or her will. Zealous attorneys decided that people shouldn't be required to take their medication. And if they wanted to be homeless, well, wasn't that their "right"? Such attorneys, in love with their own ideological rhetoric, seem unable or unwilling to see that there are human lives at risk because of their actions, the lives of people who don't have the capacity to make rational choices.

Many mentally ill people don't think they need medication. Or, if they do accept the need, medication compliance is very difficult for them. It is particularly hard for homeless people who are mentally ill. Think about it: If you're living on the streets at the survival level, do you think you could remember to take X pill at breakfast (if you even have breakfast), Y pill at lunchtime, and Z pill in the evening? Neurobiologically disordered persons on their own have a very difficult time keeping to a tight medication regimen, and if they do take their meds, they usually do so sporadically.

Once any residual effects of the medications wear off, patients may become actively psychotic. The last thing they care about is taking medications. The more psychotic they become, the less insightful they are about their problem, and thus a downward spiral of deterioration occurs. Often it's not that the families don't care; they probably don't know where the patients are and thus have no power to enforce compliance.

Sometimes the behavior of the psychotic street person becomes so bizarre or dangerous that he is involuntarily committed for a brief hospitalization—despite the best efforts of legal advocates. Doctors there evaluate the person and may place him on a good medication regimen. The person improves, the doctors give him a sheaf of prescriptions, and he is patted on the back and discharged. He may be referred to a facility where he can obtain further treatment and medication. But most homeless people don't have appointment calendars, so he may forget when he is supposed to show up at the clinic.

What also happens frequently is that the person feels better and thinks, "I don't need this medication. I'm cured." So she quits taking it. Or she forgets to take it. Without the medication, she becomes psychotic again. And the whole cyclical process begins again.

Even an ill person living in an institution can be at risk. How much greater harm can come to the mentally ill person without a home? For example, an elderly man with dementia wandered away from a nursing home in Florida and was eaten by alligators before the remains of his mutilated body were found. That incident was a rare occurrence: Most of the mentally ill homeless are victimized by other people, not by animals.

Managed Care

A more recent change that directly affects people with mental illnesses and their family caregivers is managed care. Both private health insurers and Medicaid payers try to cut back costs. Brief hospital stays are now the watchword, which means that the health insurance payer may allow patients only very limited hospital stays. In the outpatient arena, some states have tried limitations on medications for all their Medicaid patients. This has failed. The patients ended up frequenting the emergency rooms of hospitals when they became too ill to function. Nonetheless, some states continue this practice.

It is ridiculous to expect a psychotic child or adolescent to recover as quickly as a child who is not mentally ill but has a serious behavioral problem. Yet many health insurance companies lump all mental health treatment into one broad category. Thus, everyone gets a maximum number of days in the hospital (or dollars), regardless of the diagnosis. This is also true for outpatient treatment under managed care, in many cases. If you see a psychologist because your boyfriend dumped you, you are probably entitled to the same number of visits as the person whose life is nearly unbearable because of a severe obsessive-compulsive disorder.

The Media

The media, including television, radio, movies, and the theater, continue to perpetuate negative views of both the mentally ill and their families. This has been very painful for both groups and hinders the efforts of mental health professionals and the families of the mentally ill to present a true and fair portrayal of the problem.

It appears that the stereotype of the mentally ill person as evil and/or dangerous is one of the last to die—in many quarters, it is still apparently "politically correct" to deride mental illness. The good news is, however, that celebrities such as Patty Duke, Dick Cavett, and others are starting to "come out" and state that they have had serious problems or have dealt with relatives with serious mental illnesses. This is a start.

The Community Mental Health Act

In 1963, The Community Mental Health Act was introduced by President Kennedy, who had a sister who was mentally ill and developmentally delayed. Kennedy had a positive vision for mentally ill people. No longer would they be locked up and unseen by the public. Instead, they would live in nice group homes in the community. Conditions in some state hospitals were very bad. Patients were sometimes mistreated. This new vision would solve the problem, or so it was thought.

Most state hospitals would no longer be necessary. They would rapidly become dinosaurs as the system was "deinstitutionalized." The plan was that the severely mentally ill would first be placed in halfway houses and then in homes in the community. Their families could visit them, of course, when they were told they could come by the people managing the facility or the doctor.

But it didn't work out at all the way social changers imagined. In fact, E. Fuller Torrey, M.D., a psychiatrist and author whose sister has schizophrenia, says that the deinstitutionalization of the mentally ill was "the launching of a psychiatric Titanic, the largest failed social experiment of twentieth-century America."

Today, about 90 percent of the people who would have resided in mental hospitals in 1955 are not in the hospital. They are with their families or on their own. Many are homeless. Why? The halfway houses and communal homes where mentally ill people supposedly could hold jobs, live fairly normal lives in the community, and avoid the isolation and stigma of mental illness never materialized in sufficient numbers. Facilities did exist. For several decades, about 790 facilities nationwide (rather than the 2,000 proposed in the 1963 legislation) were financed by the federal government to provide care to the severely mentally ill. But many of these facilities concentrated on providing counseling for family or individual problems, rather than offering shelter or services to the severely mentally ill. Often, seriously mentally ill people were discouraged from even coming in. Some facilities used federal funds to produce nice buildings with swimming pools and swimming instructors; some even hired gardeners to keep the grounds beautiful. There was waste, and after a while, it was noticed.

In 1981, Congress killed federal funding for the centers, forcing them to fall back on state funding. Most of them closed. Again, the ill people had to go somewhere. So they went back to their families or they became homeless. Some did return to the few remaining state hospitals. The homeless population grew, as did the social costs of homelessness.

Homeless people became a trendy cause for Hollywood personalities and others who tried to convince the public that homeless people were just like "us," and that we could all be one job away from homelessness. Although apparently well intentioned, the fundraising and media attention did little to help the homeless, most of whom needed treatment for mental illness and substance abuse more than anything else.

Involuntary Hospitalization

Another change is that today it is very difficult to hospitalize a person against his will in a psychiatric facility, even when the person is floridly psychotic. In most states, mentally ill people must be a danger to themselves or others before involuntary hospitalization becomes an option, and what that means varies from state to state and even from judge to judge within a state. Why? The civil rights lawyers, again. In the early 1960s, involuntary commitments were the norm. For example, at hearings in 1961, the Superintendent of St. Elizabeth's Hospital in Washington, D.C., stated that of the 7,000 patients in the hospital, only 265 were voluntarily hospitalized. Today the situation is far different. Of an estimated 1.6 million hospital admissions (to public and private psychiatric facilities), an estimated 73 percent are voluntary admissions.

Senate committee hearings in 1961 were the turning point, and by the mid-1970s in most states patients could not be involuntarily committed to a hospital unless they were a danger to themselves or others. Of course, it should never be easy to admit people to a psychiatric facility against their will. There are family members who would take advantage of a relative who really didn't need institutional care, signing him or her in as a punishment or to get rid of the person. Ideally, a competent and ethical physician or group of physicians would commit a person for a short-term stay in a hospital. But today it is almost invariably a judge who decides when a person should be involuntarily hospitalized or ordered to take medication as an outpatient.

Once hospitalized, the next dilemma is whether the person should be required to take medication. Experts report that when the issue of medication ends up in court, judges agree with doctors in the overwhelming majority of cases; however, getting a court decision can be a lengthy process, especially if civil rights attorneys or "patient rights advocates" become involved. Meanwhile, the ill person's condition deteriorates and the risk of his doing serious bodily harm to himself or to others increases.

Movements That Oppose Medication

Another problem, although less serious than those already mentioned, is groups, predominantly the Scientologists, that vehemently oppose the use of psychiatric medications and treatments, seeing them as useless or harmful. These well-financed groups and individuals have thrown a monkey wrench into a movement toward helping mentally ill people and their families approach wellness and a chance at a happy, normal life. As of this writing, the Scientologists are attempting to outlaw electroconvulsive therapy, which has enabled many very psychotic people to improve.

The Mentally Ill Criminal

Another problem in our society is that many mentally ill people commit petty crimes or misdemeanors, either because they don't understand the laws or because they feel threatened. If you don't think fences or "no trespassing signs" apply to you, you will probably ignore them. If you think God told you to marry a particular person, you may actively pursue a romantic involvement with that person, no matter how much he or she resists your attentions.

Many mentally ill people are sent to jail for a variety of crimes, and many of the offenses are minor. They are sent to jail (and sometimes prison) with hardened criminals and they are terrified and terrorized. They may even be denied their medication. Relatives of the mentally ill inmate must struggle heroically to get anyone to address the core of the problem—mental illness.

CONCLUSION

This is the situation families face today. How can we function in this environment? It is possible, if you know some of the intricacies and "tricks" that other families have learned: how to get your ill relative into a hospital; how to get her to take the medication that makes her rational, or nearly so. It is also true that most psychiatrists today espouse the neurobiological model and are eager to learn as much as possible about the many new medications that are being introduced.

Today more than ever families have the opportunity to gain information about neurobiological disorders and their effects on ill people. By identifying competent and caring mental health professionals and teaming with them to help the ill person and the family, caregivers are empowered. This is my wish for you.

2

LIVING WITH THE ILLNESS

Why would anyone choose to live with a mentally ill person? Wouldn't you have to be mentally ill yourself to make such a voluntary choice? Not at all. People choose to live with a mentally ill person (also known as a "neurobiologically disordered" person), for some very valid reasons. Perhaps it is because that person is your own much-loved child, as in my family's case. Or maybe the person is a parent, a brother, a sister, a spouse. Contrary to the generally held belief that most mentally ill people live in institutions, the majority (an estimated 50 to 70 percent) of the millions of mentally ill people in the United States and Canada live at home with their families.

The mentally ill come in all ages: Some are aging and suffer from dementia and are cared for by a spouse or an adult child or sibling. Others are young, in the prime of life and health but, for example, they can't work because they're afraid to leave the house. Still others are adolescents and children, racked with the pain of major depression, obsessive-compulsive disorder (OCD), Tourette's syndrome, anxiety disorder, schizophrenia, or some other serious neurobiological disorder. In addition, people of all ages suffer from a combination of illnesses; for example, a person with schizophrenia may also be clinically depressed. It is undoubtedly terribly hard to be a mentally ill person, to suffer from the anxiety of feeling persecuted or to experience the anguish of trying to escape the voices in your head. But it's also extremely hard to be an emotionally well person and see this illness every day in someone you love. Normal coping skills often fail. You can become sick or depressed yourself, your work can suffer, and your marriage could even fail because of the stress.

MY STORY

Signing my 12-year-old daughter into a psychiatric hospital was the single most heartwrenching and difficult thing I've ever done. She'd become increasingly sick, but she did have enough grounding in reality to report that she was spinning out of control and felt suicidal. Talking hadn't helped, therapy hadn't helped, nothing had helped. I felt that her life was in danger, and the psychiatrist my pediatrician had referred us to was insisting that Jane be admitted to the hospital for her own safety.

So I sat there and signed paper after paper, not sure if I was doing the right thing, not sure what *was* the right thing at all. I asked the doctor if they used shock treatment on their patients and she seemed greatly offended as she told me, no, they definitely did *not* use electroconvulsive therapy in this facility. I didn't know if that was good or bad. My images of a psychiatric hospital were blends of an old movie in which Olivia DeHaviland was confined in the awful "Snake Pit" institution, a visit to the state hospital for a college psychology course, and pieces of novels and books. It all added up to something nightmarish—except it was all too terrifyingly real.

Jane wanted to go into the hospital because she thought maybe they could help her, so she didn't protest at all. She didn't cry, she didn't seem to react in any way. But I cried. When I left her, I cried all the way home. Had I done the right thing? Would she be all right? Would they be able to help her? What if they hurt her or abused her—how did I know that she was really and truly safe? What I didn't know then was that the hospital staff would ultimately stabilize her, but that there were no quick fixes, then or now. And there would be many more anguished days and nights ahead until we came to terms with the fact that our daughter was mentally ill. And even afterwards.

Two years before, a psychologist had told me Jane was probably suffering from schizophrenia and should be on medication. She explained that it was a problem with thinking and that it was due to a chemical imbalance. She recommended that Jane see a psychiatrist and be placed on medication, and I followed her advice.

Jane was fine for nearly a year, but then the deterioration began. People were whispering about her—or so she said. Kids were being "mean" to her. I took her to another psychologist, who said she needed to be with other kids. It was summertime, and with the psychologist's strong approval, I enrolled her in a day camp.

Jane lasted several weeks. Every day when it was time to go home, she'd rush to my side as soon as I arrived and she'd tell me the others were awful, they "made fun of" her, and she hated the day camp. Then one day, the camp counselor called me and told me to come get Jane, right away. She was cringing in a corner and sobbing. They said, come get her and do *not* come back. I rushed to the day camp and Jane was greatly relieved to see me. Her eyes and face were red and the counselors looked grim. How could I explain it to them? I did not understand what was going on myself. She calmed down as soon as she got in the car with me and was fine the rest of the day. I was not fine.

The next milestone we faced was that Jane was about to enter seventh grade, a new school after seven years in her elementary school (grades K–6). Would she be able to handle such a transition? The psychologist talked to her weekly, and her father and I tried to build up the school in positive terms, but Jane became increasingly fearful.

School began and Jane became "sick" frequently. She called me to say she had a headache, a stomachache, a pain somewhere. The doctor could find no medical problem. Then one day, she was particularly distraught because some students had (supposedly) criticized her behavior. I say "supposedly" because she also suffered from paranoia, and sometimes imagined persecutions. She had become hysterical. I came to the office to pick her up. While I was there, the secretary asked me why I had paid for a whole month of lunches but Jane had not eaten a single lunch. Afterwards, I learned that at lunchtime, Jane had walked around outside the cafeteria, afraid to go in. She didn't know where to sit or whom to sit with, so it seemed safer to stay outside. People at the school office knew this but they did not tell me, apparently assuming that I was aware of this behavior and approved of it. Of course, I was not and did not.

Things got worse. Jane seemed to be slipping further and further from reality; in fact, she asked me how I knew that I was "real." Shaken, I took her to the pediatrician, who urged me to obtain immediate psychiatric help.

During Jane's first hospitalization (which was about six weeks long), my father-in-law became precipitously and critically ill with cancer. It was emotionally wrenching for my husband, who drove to visit his father every day after work and to see our daughter on every visiting day. (Psychiatric hospitals typically do not allow daily visits.) And then my father-in-law died. You are not exempt from other life problems and stresses when someone in your family becomes mentally ill.

Meanwhile, Jane was getting worse in the hospital. She started eating with her hands and exhibited other behavior she had never shown before. She wanted makeup and when she was denied this, she put large amounts of talcum powder on her face. She cringed when older children looked at her or came anywhere near her. When we came to visit her, she averted her eyes and acted bored. We told her that her grandfather was sick. She didn't care. These are just a few examples of her troubling behavior. The staff members at the hospital periodically called me and asked me what I did when Jane did this or that and I would tell them that she had never done these things before. Eventually, however, she did stabilize and was released back into our care.

There were improvements and there were severe relapses. Jane was hospitalized again about a year later. She also went through "day treatment" as a hospital outpatient, during which she spent the day in the hospital and returned home each night for several weeks. There was also a time when she could not attend school for several months because she was so sick. Jane became my shadow. If I needed to go to the supermarket, she wanted to go, too. She always had to know where I was. I became very anxious.

Yet, there were good times, too. At one point, Jane was doing so well that she was to be "mainstreamed" back into regular school classes and out of the "emotionally handicapped" classes she had entered in grade seven after the first hospitalization. First, she would have to be in a transitional classroom, which I was assured was a wonderful opportunity for Jane. It sounded great.

But this experiment turned out to be a disaster. The one other girl in her class was nearly catatonic—she would not speak unless directly addressed by a teacher. The boys were all severe behavior problems. Jane struggled to cope in this environment. Then one day, a boy in her class told Jane that she was "ugly." I don't know if he really said this to her or she imagined it. But her reaction was to run out of the school and across the street, where she found some broken glass. She cut her arms and legs until the blood flowed. She felt no pain, a common schizophrenic symptom. She did not feel real. The voices demanded that she do it, and she complied. I drove her straight to the hospital after this incident, calling ahead to let them know we were en route.

How is Jane as of this writing? Now she is on a powerful antipsychotic medication called Clozaril. She gets a blood test once a week to ensure that she has not developed the rare (and fatal) blood disease that occurs in less than 2 percent of the people who have taken this medication. The lab faxes the results to the pharmacy, and I obtain one more week's supply of the drug for Jane.

Jane now feels "real," she thinks logically most of the time, and she is coming back to a world that had been lost to her for years. In fact, when the doctor asked her if she felt better, she said she knew she was better because she knew she was real and really here, not out in space somewhere. I compare Jane to Dr. Manette in *A Tale of Two Cities*. As Dr. Manette was locked in his cell in the Bastille, so was Jane imprisoned by her own mind. Dr. Manette regained his sanity and freedom, and his recovery process was titled "Recalled to Life"— a most appropriate phrase for what happened to Jane.

Jane is much better, but still struggles every day with her illness, which causes her to have memory problems, problems with physical coordination, and a hypersensitivity to what others say. But she is so vastly improved that it is miraculous. If Jane stays at her current level of functioning, that would be wonderful. The problem with many mental illnesses, however, is that no matter how effective the medication is or how caring her family, friends, and teachers are, sometimes relapses do occur. My husband and children know this and we keep it in the back of our minds.

I've described my experience with caring for a mentally ill person. But what is it like for you?

HOW DOES IT FEEL AT FIRST?

How does it feel when a much-loved family member becomes mentally ill? Can words convey the gut-wrenching horror of it all, of seeing your once beautiful and happy relative become a tormented being who imagines that people are whispering terrible things about her? How does it feel to watch as her personal hygiene falls apart and she refuses to bathe or wash her hair?

Suppose the mentally ill person is your spouse. How does it feel when his behavior in public sometimes *does* make people look at him and whisper about him, thus confirming his paranoia? He's an adult; he's supposed to act, well, "adult." It's embarrassing when he doesn't. But if you tell people that he has a mental illness, often they will cringe in fear. Or they may laugh nervously.

Suppose the mentally ill person is your parent, a loving mother or father, who now has Alzheimer's disease or some other psychiatric problem. Since our parents cared for and loved us, do we owe them years of devoted care? And what if the elderly person is petulant, even unpleasant? It's a shocking and painful change for most adult children, and the decisions about whether to provide care, as well as what care is to be provided, are tough to make.

An Emotional Roller-Coaster Ride

Actually, being a caregiver to a mentally ill person is much harder than a roller-coaster ride. A roller-coaster ride is something you embark on willingly, even if, in the middle of the ride, you wonder why you did it. And there is an end to it—it's only a brief ride and you don't have to get on again. But it's the best analogy I can think of for being a caregiver to a mentally ill person. There are high peaks and deep valleys and sometimes you have no idea what is over the next rise. Will she be in a good mood? Will his demons threaten him?

If you provide care to a child or adult who is blind, the person is not blind one day, seeing the next, somewhat visually impaired the next, and so on. But the caregivers of mentally ill people face this kind of uncertainty about their loved one's condition every day. Sometimes they see big improvements in the mentally ill person. Sometimes they only imagine big improvements because they want so much for this person to be well. And then there are times when the person relapses, thus distressing the caregiver whose hopes are again dashed, especially if he or she does not realize that relapses sometimes happen.

COMMON CAREGIVER REACTIONS TO THE ILLNESS

Caregivers face a broad array of problems and experience many emotional responses to them. Before you can become even remotely effective at coping with your own feelings, you need to start by recognizing and accepting that your relative is mentally ill. This is inevitably a painful experience for you and your family. Although not all caregivers react in the same way, common reactions include self-blame, grief, feeling overloaded, and guilt. Many families deny for a long time that there is a problem at all, because it is too painful to believe. (See Chapter 3 for a discussion of the steps leading to acceptance of the illness.) You may also suffer physical reactions such as headaches, stomachaches, and other medical problems. Don't ignore them: Get medical treatment.

Emotional Reactions

SELF-BLAMING AND GUILT

One reason for the guilt and self-blame caregivers experience is the terrible stigma of mental illness, a stigma that extends to non–mentally ill family members. It is a form of guilt by association. According to a 1990 survey of attitudes of the general public toward the mentally ill, performed by the National Institute of Mental Health, 71 percent of the individuals surveyed believed that mental illness was caused by emotional weakness, 65 percent believed that mental illness was caused by bad parenting; and 43 percent believed that mentally ill people caused their own illness. None of this is true, but it is what people believe.

Self-blame is a common reaction among caregivers, almost a universal reaction at first. Sometimes it remains in the background, like elevator music that you don't quite hear. Parents blame themselves. Siblings think it was something they did. One woman cried as she told me that for years she had thought she had made her schizophrenic sister sick because she had jumped on her stomach when they were playing one day. Nobody had ever told her that it wasn't her fault.

Spouses wonder if they were not understanding enough or if somehow they drove the person "to the edge." One woman's husband suffered from terrible mood swings (and was later diagnosed with manic depression). He attributed them all to her actions. She later learned that she was not responsible for the violent changes in her husband's moods and said, "If he says, 'I don't feel good because you were watching the wrong channel on TV last night,' it doesn't bother me anymore."

Of all the questions I asked people who are caregivers to mentally ill children and adults, the one question that truly shocked them was: "What do you think you have done that was right?" So many seemed programmed to accentuate their errors and mistakes and possible wrongdoings that it was actually difficult for them to consider what positive things they had done. This is tragic, considering the years of hard work, compassion, and care that families have provided. Once they thought about it, most of the people told me that "hanging in there" and continuing to love and fight for the ill person was the most important and the best thing they did.

FEELING OVERLOADED

Feeling overwhelmed and overloaded is common. A study by Edward H. Thompson, Jr. and William Doll, reported in a 1982 issue of *Family Relations,* revealed that 72 percent of caregivers to patients who were discharged from the state mental hospital and returned home felt overloaded and burdened by their caregiving role. They were emotionally drained by the demands on them. Of these, about 45 percent felt "moderately" burdened while 27 percent felt "severely" burdened.

GRIEF AND SORROW

Overwhelming sadness, grief, and sorrow over the loss of the healthy person you once knew is a common reaction, one you have probably experienced, too. And it's not a grief that is resolved and then forgotten. Instead, the grief can crop up periodically and be just as painful and present as it was the first time. If you know this and accept it as a normal reaction, you will be able to cope with it better. Psychiatric instructor Kris McLoughlin, in *Neurobiological Disorders in Children and Adolescents*, says,

Chronic grieving best describes the reactions of families whose children have a serious NBD. [Neurobiological disorder, which refers to a chemical imbalance in the brain and which causes severe mental illnesses.] In my experience with such families, it is not uncommon to see feelings of guilt, anger, despair, and shock emerge, subside, and reemerge. Professionals should understand and accept this ongoing process, and they should help the family cope with both the erratic course of the child's illness and the waxing-and-waning nature of the family's grief.

This passage applies equally well to caregivers of mentally ill adults.

Mental illness is also a kind of "psychosocial loss," not only for the ill person but also for the family and society at large. What might the person have achieved had mental illness not invaded his or her life? Caregivers can't help wondering this.

In addition, families grieve the loss of the person they once knew: Often, mentally ill people do not evince symptoms until adolescence or adulthood. As a result, the family has known the person as a functioning and healthy individual. They want that person back and they grieve over that person's disappearance. What they suffer is a kind of "disenfranchised grief." The person is not dead, is not even terminally ill. There are no rites or ceremonies to provide an outlet for grief and help the family accept the loss. But the person they once knew is gone, maybe forever. A loved spouse—lost to mental illness. A beloved sibling—lost to mental illness. A cherished child—lost to mental illness.

Not only do people grieve over the loss of the person they knew, but they also grieve over the radical change in their lifestyles. They may lose touch with friends and be unable to participate in formerly enjoyed activities. (See Chapter 7 on the importance of taking care of yourself.)

FIXATING ON THE PAST

Atkinson wrote about the "myth of the 'before' person" as a problem that many families have difficulty getting beyond. They may idealize the person the relative was before he became ill and long for him to return to a status he never really had. Says Atkinson, "It seems that many families have an extra member, the 'ghost of patient past.'

Coupled with the idealized 'ghost of patient future,' the patient of the present could be seen as occupying an insignificant family role."

Because the family so intensely longs for the patient to be like she was "before," they may not recognize or acknowledge the very real gains that the ill individual makes. To do so, they need to realize that the person of the past is gone, and the person that exists now is the one who needs to be accepted and dealt with. Says Atkinson, "A role must be found in the family for the patient as he is; affection, if it is given, must be given for him as he is now, and not with the qualifications of a former personality to be attained, or merely because of that former personality."

If it is your child who is now ill, those dreams of him growing up to become a brain surgeon or her becoming a famous author—or even an average happy person—will have to be put away, or at least put on hold. If it is your parent who is ill, you may experience a role reversal in which your parent relates to you childishly, as if you were the parent. As a result, although still physically present, that comforting parental figure you may have relied on in the past is gone forever.

Anyone would be upset by these losses. What you need to do is figure out how to accept your feelings and work toward a resolution. One book I find helpful is *Grieving Mental Illness: A Guide for Patients and Their Caregivers*, written by Virginia Lafond, a person with the unique experiences of being a mental health professional *and* having been mentally ill herself.

SHOCK

Although your relative's mental functioning may have been diminishing, it could have been so gradual that it was hardly noticeable. When the realization hits, it can be very shocking. For example, you may have a parent or even a spouse with a mild case of Alzheimer's. But this person is functioning at a high and acceptable level. Then the person becomes ill, with pneumonia or a hip fracture, or another problem requiring hospitalization. The deterioration can accelerate rapidly and become very apparent to the family.

Says David Sudderth, M.D., a neurologist with the Neurology Center of Naples in Naples, Florida, "It is especially in this setting that the family becomes distraught. 'What have you done to my husband/father?' screams the family to the nurses and doctors. 'He was fine until he came here!'" Dr. Sudderth says that actually the person was not fine, but was still able to use the minimal skills he or she had. "Until Ma stops cleaning or cooking or gets pneumonia, she might not get diagnosed!" says Sudderth. "However, if people had been asking her what day it is, checking her memory, speech/language function, she could not have escaped diagnosis."

If a person becomes psychotic within a short period, especially someone who has been away at college or working away from home, the discovery that he is mentally ill is a terrible shock to parents and other family members back home. It just doesn't seem to make any sense; it is difficult to believe. And yet, it happens. One parent discovered her son was sick when he was found walking the streets of New York City stark naked.

It can be a sick feeling, right in your gut, to be hit with the realization that a cherished loved one is mentally ill. Acknowledging these feelings is a step toward the acceptance you need to attain. Not passivity, but acceptance of a tough problem that you'll be involved in—probably for the long term.

FEELING ALONE OR HOPELESS

We caregivers often feel terribly alone and isolated, as if we have been deserted on an island. Depression can accompany all the other emotions.

"You just don't even feel like going out sometimes," says S., the caregiver of a mentally ill woman. "You really have to force yourself to see your friends, and even if you do have someone available to watch her [her daughter], you wonder if it's really worth it. So, too often, you just stay home. You feel like no one understands."

People who attend family support group meetings almost invariably report that they are amazed and heartened to learn that others have suffered with the same or similar problems. It is truly a healing revelation. They also learn the importance of creating a social life apart from the ill person.

EMBARRASSMENT AND SHAME

You may feel ashamed by the ill person's behavior in public. You may be extremely uncomfortable if the person continually spills food, looks frantically around a room, feels compelled to touch things or count them, or exhibits other behavior that is not "normal."

You may also feel ashamed of expressing your own fears. Hey, what are *you* complaining about? It's not *you* who is mentally ill; it's your family member who is suffering so horribly. But you need to recognize that you *are* suffering, too. It is painful to watch someone you love suffer, a kind of vicarious torture.

One parent reported that her daughter, who became psychotic as an adult, has recovered a great deal of her functioning and she has married and has a child. She cannot work—work is far too stressful, but she has achieved a high level of success. But the ill woman's husband has decreed that his parents must never find out about her previous hospitalizations for psychiatric illness. It would be too horrible, too embarrassing. So the woman (and her mother) must keep the secret, sharing the shame and feeling guilty—for something neither of them had any control over. This is one example of how not to act. It would be far better if the woman and her daughter convinced the husband there should be no shame attached to her previous illness. The bottom line is that often you *will* feel embarrassed or ashamed, but as you learn to accept these feelings, they generally diminish.

FEAR

If you are the biological relative of a mentally ill person, you may fear it will also happen to *you*, whether it's Alzheimer's disease, schizophrenia, or some other serious mental illness. It appears that there are genetic predispositions to many (if not all) mental illnesses, so this fear is valid and should be discussed openly. Hiding it in the back of your mind is not good for you. Talk to a psychiatrist or social worker about risk probabilities for relatives.

Some caregivers are also fearful of the mentally ill person, who may be much stronger than they are and may have difficulty controlling his anger. (Generally, it is males who lash out physically, although females may do so, too.) These are problems that must be dealt with. You must not allow yourself to be abused. And if that sometimes means calling the police to protect you against your son, daughter, husband, wife, or any other relative or acquaintance, then you must steel yourself to do it. (See Chapter 7 for further information.)

The family, including siblings, often worries about what will happen in the future. Parents wonder who will care for their neurobiologically disordered child when they die. Siblings wonder if they will be expected to care for the person, and may secretly dread the thought of this future burden. Such issues must be discussed up front with the family. There are many aspects to this fear: Where will the person live? Who will see that he or she takes medication? Who will love the person? These issues are discussed further in Part Two, but it's important to state here that fear can only be combated with knowledge and planning (see Chapter 14).

ANGER

Sometimes you may wonder if other people are right and the relative isn't really *that* sick. Couldn't this person just try a little harder? Are you perhaps coddling him? (And in some cases, you may be right.) Said one mother, who reported on her experiences to a Florida newspaper, "First, we blamed her. Why couldn't she shape up? She needed to apply herself more. . . . Then, naturally, we blamed ourselves. Her father and I had divorced, so we were an excellent target, and began to assume the guilt that society was eager to lay on us." This mother later learned that her daughter suffered from schizophrenia, which most professionals now agree is caused by a chemical imbalance in the brain.

Physical Reactions

When you learn that your relative is mentally ill, you may experience some short-term, and possible long-term, physical ailments. Many systems of your body can become involved; for example, you may experience sleeplessness that is directly related to worry and fear. You may also have a change in appetite, either eating much more or much less than you normally would. Women may have menstrual problems or an irregular cycle. You may feel exhausted. You may have gastrointestinal problems, such as diarrhea or stomachaches. If you previously had a medical problem, you may find it flaring up under the stress you are experiencing.

Such physical reactions to the grief and stress that accompany the realization that your relative is mentally ill are common; however, do seek medical help because you don't want to ignore any underlying medical problems that can be resolved. Be sure to tell your physician about the stress you are under, but ask your doctor to determine what, if anything, you can do to improve your health.

LOOKING FOR SOMEONE TO BLAME

The "Mom Did It" Myth

Until fairly recently, mothers of autistic children and mothers of children and adults with schizophrenia were called "refrigerator" or "schizophrenegenic" mothers. These terms were used by Freudian psychoanalysts to explain the causes of schizophrenia or autism and laid the blame squarely at the allegedly cold and unfeeling mother's feet. She was said to have made her child mentally ill by her behavior. If the child was autistic, she was overinvolved and smothering.

Another aspect of this harmful and false theory was that mothers supposedly constantly gave children two mutually exclusive goals or indicated mutually exclusive feelings—a "double bind." A simple example would be "Come here" and "Go away," at the same time. Since the child could not fulfill both of the orders, he or she supposedly had a psychotic break. An emotional double bind would be if the mother said "I love you," while furiously frowning and gesticulating anger.

Psychiatrists with these views perceived children as "blank slates" on which mothers imprinted beliefs and behavior. Thus, the attitude was, if the child is psychotic, well, you've had the child all these years, you must have done it, Mom. Most psychiatrists no longer believe this although, sadly, there are still those who do. Thus, if a person suffers from psychotic depression, panic attacks, anxiety, phobias, or virtually any other serious mental illness, then somebody in the family (probably Mom) must have done something to the person. That was the theory.

Even psychiatrists who are personally and directly affected by mental illness can become entrapped in this mindset. One of my interviewees was a psychoanalyst and a mother whose own daughter became mentally ill. She found that mental health professionals blamed her when her daughter became ill, and she herself wondered what she might have done to cause this problem. (And she still has some vestigial guilt.) She also blamed her ex-husband. His frequent absences must have been the cause, or at least a contributing factor. But what she ultimately came to believe was that she had been a good mother and her ex-husband had done his best. The illness happened for some other reason. Said this psychiatrist/mother, somewhat wryly, "Mother gets the blame for everything and the credit for nothing. I always tell my patients that—that's the way our society works."

Even when the neurobiology of mental illness is ultimately acknowledged, there is still a lot of residual pain felt by families who have been chastised for years that it's "all your fault." Sometimes families are even criticized by their ill relative, whose psychiatrist conveyed this misinformation. According to one book for mental health professionals,

> Devoted families who endured waves of self-recrimination and criticism from professionals and who made massive sacrifices in an effort to purge the germ in their life have had to face the realization that all that careful self-scrutiny may have been for naught. The effect is equivalent to being released from prison after 10 years and told that you never committed the crime, that it was all a mistake. (From *Families as Allies in Treatment of the Mentally Ill: New Directions for Mental Health Professionals*, American Psychiatric Press, Inc., 1990.)

A New Villain: Fathers

Today many mental health professionals have begun to shun the idea that the problems of the mentally ill person are all Mom's fault. How retro, how passé, how unfair! Now some therapists have come up with Dad as the "true" culprit. He's absent from the home or absent too much. He's not nurturing enough or he's overnurturing. He stimulates the child by walking around in his underwear on Saturday. The bottom line is that he can't do anything right.

In fact, maybe he sexually abused the child. This is the secret fear of many fathers—that they will be wrongfully accused of sexual abuse by a therapist who identifies all mental illness with sexual aberrations. Of course it is true that some fathers or other males in the family do or have sexually abused children. But most people would question the remembered abuse of an adult who says she was abused as a three-month-old infant.

In any case, even if the father did abuse the person as a child, experts say this cannot cause a neurobiological disorder. It could make the person neurotic and cause severe personal and interpersonal problems. But rarely could it cause a continuous psychosis. If a therapist immediately sees sexual abuse as the sole cause of an illness such as schizophrenia, manic depression, or other severe mental illness, you need to hire a new therapist or at least get another opinion. Don't presume that an allegation is true—or untrue. Investigate it.

Self-Blame

Because of this long-held presumption by mental health professionals that the mother and/or the dysfunctional family has made the ill person sick, many caregivers have suffered horribly. By accepting the blame, they may then believe that they deserve to suffer too, as atonement for their misdeeds—even if they can't figure out what those misdeeds were. So they will let the ill person verbally or physically abuse them; they will spend inordinate stretches of time struggling to help the ill person and trudging from one mental health professional to another; they'll sacrifice their entire lives to the ill person. This is a tragic mistake.

The Unfairness of It All

One of my interviewees was the father of a mentally ill son who is now nineteen, and has just moved out. He realized his son was mentally ill about three years ago, and says he felt confused and scared, which probably came out as anger, even though he was not angry. The main reaction was confusion and fear. "*Why* is this happening to us?" It just wasn't fair.

It is *not* fair that your loved one has a mental illness and that you must deal with it. It is hard to think of what your parent, child, or spouse could have been (or was) and it really hurts. But it is a fact of life that people learn to deal with and that you, too, can eventually accept.

Views from Experts on Caregivers'
Emotional Reactions

Marge Lenane is a Licensed Clinical Social Worker (LCSW) and Project Coordinator of the Childhood Onset of Schizophrenia project at the National Institute for Mental Health in Bethesda, Maryland.

This is a valuable research project, and the only one of its kind in the world, to try to find the causes of schizophrenia in children.

Lenane often sees two common initial emotional responses when a parent learns of a child's mental illness. "Probably the first two emotional responses are denial and pain. Understandably, parents do not want to believe that their child is different from the child they had hoped for," says Lenane.

Researchers say that for many, it is almost as if there has been a death in the family, even though no one has died. What has died instead, as alluded to earlier, is the dream future that every parent has for a child. Says Gary Mosher, M.D., a psychiatrist with Circles of Care in Merritt Island, Florida, "The family had aspirations or hopes for that mentally ill member and now they're reorganizing those goals and aspirations."

THE STIGMATIZED FAMILY

The overall societal attitude toward mental illness makes the caregiver's burden much heavier. Says Nancy J. Herman, a sociologist and researcher at the Central Michigan University in Mount Pleasant, Michigan, who has studied American and Canadian families of the mentally ill since 1978, "One very big problem was what I call the 'courtesy stigma.' Nearly 95 percent of the families I've studied felt that the stigma of a family member's mental illness was extended to them, by virtue of association," says Herman.

So what did the family tell people about the ill person? Usually nothing. "They spent a great deal of their time trying to cover up and hide it from the neighbors, with stories that Uncle Harry was off on a five-year trip around the world." The effort that goes into these lies takes a tremendous toll on families. It's not worth it. Don't do it.

Another tactic, says Herman, was to prevent people from visiting, and she cites the son or daughter who would always meet their friends on the front porch and never let them in the house, "even when it was below zero—because they were scared that their friends would see their mentally ill father."

Some family members would rarely go out or rarely take the mentally ill person out. "Or they'd go to another town where no one knew them. They used very elaborate strategies," says Herman. Yet this behavior perpetuates the stigma, and it becomes an endless cycle as these families bow their heads in shame. This cycle must be broken by families.

It's not just their imagination that they may be rejected if they speak out. One mother whose adult son became ill with schizophrenia while in college reported that her relatives had always enjoyed bringing their friends to the library concerts her son gave. They bragged about him and were thrilled to have some association with this gifted performer. "But when he got sick, then they didn't know him and they didn't want to know us anymore. They just dropped us," said his mother.

THE CAREGIVING "PLAYERS"

Overburdened Females

Ironically, the person who has been the most blamed usually serves as the primary caregiver: the mother, wife, or sister. Very often it is still a female in the family who takes over the bulk of the emotional and physical work. Even while at work, she may receive calls from the ill person or others who are concerned with the ill person such as doctors and social workers. The caregiving burden may not let up, and there's no relief in sight.

Yet there are rudimentary (and pretty rare) forms of respite in some areas; for example, day care centers for adults who are mentally impaired. Some corporations provide advice for families with children or adults with problems, usually with an emphasis on the elderly. Some support groups may also work out a plan whereby you provide care for someone's relative now and you will be provided care for your relative later, a kind of babysitting cooperative. These take work to put together! And yet they are so necessary for exhausted caregivers.

The Family and Medical Leave Act allows for time off from work (up to 12 weeks) for a caregiver who needs to care for a child, elderly parent, or spouse. Unfortunately, these are unpaid weeks, so most people cannot afford to take the maximum amount of time off.

It should also be noted that there is an "up" side to caregiving for relatives; for example, researchers have found that such caregiving provides families with a new appreciation of each other and even an altered perception of life and family. One mother said that for the first time in a long time, she felt very close to her grown daughter, as they worked together to clean her mother's home.

Effect on Other Family Members

Beyond the primary caregiver are other people directly involved in and affected by the person's mental illness, usually other family members. They can stop thinking about the problem for long periods, as they work and pursue other interests. But it's still in the back of their minds and it's still worrying them. And when the ill person becomes worse, they are deeply affected.

They may distance themselves from the person with the neurobiological disorder and concentrate instead on their activities with the outside world as a sort of survival mechanism. They may also avoid the primary caregiver because of her deep involvement with the ill person. Spouses may become angry with wives who are caregivers. (See Chapter 9 for information on caregiving of spouses.)

Effect on Other Relatives

A "third tier" of involvement is usually the extended family, the people who don't live with the family. These are grandparents, aunts and uncles, adult siblings, and others. In one case, a caregiving mother had to battle her mother-in-law, who insisted that the ill person was just fine and did not need medication or hospitalization. This was very stressful and bewildering for the young woman with the neurobiological disorder, as it was for her loving mother who already had to cope with the initial trauma of having an adult child with a mental illness.

CONCLUSION

I would like to leave you at the end of this chapter with this thought: The more frequently that families of mentally ill people speak out, rather than hanging our heads in shame, the more we can work together on eradicating the stigma of mental illness and effectively help our families and ourselves. The more we educate ourselves about our relative's illness, the more we free ourselves. Knowledge is truly power.

3

ACCEPTING THE ILLNESS

Accepting the fact of your relative's illness isn't easy. The process can be very painful and there are often setbacks during which, for example, you again deny the problem, search for possible causes, and so forth. This may occur when the person has a relapse, thus causing reanalysis of the problem and setting in motion all that agonizing soul searching again.

Phases of acceptance may not occur in the exact order described here. Thus, readers should not conclude that you start with A, then B, move to the end, and stop. With these caveats, I'll describe the phases of acceptance.

PHASES OF ACCEPTANCE

You will probably pass through various stages before accepting that your relative is truly mentally ill. First, you may notice some odd behavior that you can't understand, but you explain it away. You and other family members convince yourselves that it's temporary, it's just a "stage," and it'll go away. But then something happens that jolts you and makes you think that this is *not* just a stage, this is a serious problem. The ill person's behavior may have deteriorated or an outside party, perhaps a teacher or a physician, may alert the family.

Things get worse. Finally, you must admit, completely, that your relative has a serious problem. The person is admitted to a psychiatric hospital or drops out of school and won't leave his room. Yet you may still believe that the problem is temporary.

Parents try to figure out where they went wrong. Mothers may go through old photo albums staring at pictures of the ill person as a child, looking for a trace of psychosis or unhappiness. Spouses wonder what they may have done to "set off" the person. Siblings think they may have caused the problem. Everyone is walking on eggs. You don't know what to do. You may be demoralized and upset, with no idea where to go from here. What you need is education and support—but you may not know this yet. You feel totally alone and don't think anyone out there knows how you feel. You're wrong. Others do know.

DON'T DENY THE ILLNESS

Many people initially deny that their relative is mentally ill, despite what the experts tell them. This is a serious problem, because if you don't think your relative needs help, then you won't seek it out. The ill person may become much worse and could even cause harm to himself or to you. Denial is a stage of grief. People often deny other painful problems, such as the death of a beloved person or the new knowledge of a serious illness, as well. Denial can last for years— people can be very good at fooling themselves that it's not really mental illness, because the truth is too painful to face. And yet, to effectively cope with mental illness in your family, you need to acknowledge that truth.

Neil Lombardi, M.D., a pediatric neurologist and vice president of medical services for St. Mary's Hospital for Children in Bayside, New York, says, "A good proportion of families deny it right off. The resistance to going and seeking psychiatric help is a big problem." Maybe you are afraid that if you take your relative to a psychiatrist, he or she will be locked up immediately. Or you may have irrational fears of psychiatrists. Popular books and movies often depict psychiatrists as evil beings, thus magnifying people's fears. You need to overcome such fears. (Finding a competent physician is covered in Chapter 4.)

Although it's very important for families to seek out information, you need to know that there is rarely one "quick fix" solution to virtually any type of mental illness. There are medications that help greatly and therapy can also help—but neither will eradicate the illness. Research seems to indicate that effective medication and good therapy are the best combination that helps the ill person, followed by medication only, and, dead last, therapy only.

Accept That Mentally Ill People Will Behave Irrationally

Although a mentally ill person generally does not behave irrationally in every aspect of her life, she will certainly exhibit some irrational behavior. Once you begin to accept that a mentally ill person will sometimes behave irrationally, you alleviate some of your own internal stress and strain. For example, a paranoid person really does believe that people are talking about him, and it does you no good to try to convince him otherwise. He *knows* that it is happening. Or his voices tell him so. (See Chapter 8 for further information on this problem.)

The main point in accepting that irrationality is consistent with mental illness is that once you do so you can begin to develop more effective coping mechanisms. No longer burdened by the "what-ifs" or "shoulds" in your mind, you can deal with the way things really are. And you seek out what works.

DEALING WITH YOUR OWN DAY-TO-DAY PROBLEMS

When the Ill Person Is Your Child

One major error many spouses make when they care for a mentally ill child is to place all or nearly all of the caregiving burden on one person. Everyone needs a break, and it's important that the burden, if not shared 50/50, be spread out more equitably than 100/0. The stress that is generated by living with a mentally ill person can be extremely deleterious to the happiest marriages.

One mother of three children told me that when her son became mentally ill, her husband told her that he would take care of the two well children and she could care for the ill one. However, caregiving for a mentally ill child does not equal the work involved in caregiving for two well children. These parents worked things out, but the marriage nearly failed because of the father's intransigence.

Marge Lenane, a licensed clinical social worker and project coordinator of the Childhood Onset of Schizophrenia project at the National Institute for Mental Health in Bethesda, Maryland, says that it's critically important for caregivers to take care of a marital relationship when they are caring for a mentally ill family member. "If they don't nurture that relationship, then the relationship may not be there to provide the stability the child needs."

So don't blame each other for your child's mental problems or argue over treatment. Don't ignore your relationship with your spouse and give all your attention to the ill child. It's difficult to go through this experience alone; it is far better to face it together. It's easy to get distracted by careers or other aspects of life, but that won't solve the problem; it will just make things worse. Face the difficult problem of mental illness in all of its ramifications, and face it together.

When the Ill Person Is Your Spouse

If the ill person is your spouse, your whole marital balance shifts. In studies of families with a depressed spouse, stress levels within the family are primarily affected when the ill person is symptomatic. One woman said she felt very conflicted because she was an ardent feminist—so why was she putting up with this mentally ill husband who was so difficult to live with? "There's this part that says, hey, if you're in a bad relationship, get out of it. But I couldn't get out of this one. It was a combination of loving him and feeling bound to take care of him. I didn't know if he could survive on his own," she said.

You might think that it would help if you bring in a relative to assist with caregiving, for example, your mother-in-law. Not so. Bringing in a third party is very risky for the marriage because it may create a wedge between the husband and wife and drive them apart. With a third party in the family, the ill person tends to become more dependent and isolated. But when a family handles the problems within itself, it is more likely to survive, although it won't be easy.

A couple's sex life may also be affected. The depressed person may lose interest in sex; or the person with manic depression may want more sex while in a manic state. In addition, medications can affect libido. If this happens, talk to the doctor, who may have some suggestions. Don't be embarrassed.

Lastly, a key factor in maintaining a marital relationship with a spouse who is mentally ill is to separate the person from the disease. Even if it is difficult, try your best to see your spouse as attractive. If you can maintain your love for the ill person, then your relationship has a good chance of surviving.

When the Ill Person Is Your Parent

Often there is tension and conflict between relatives of caregivers, particularly if the ill person is a parent. The primary caregiver may believe that he or she is the "good" person, while the others who aren't providing caregiving are the uncaring relatives. Intense family disagreements may develop if such issues are not brought out up front.

In addition, former roles may be reenacted. The "big sister" may tell the "baby brother" that she'll handle this problem—even though the baby brother is a 40-year-old professional who is quite competent to provide some assistance. As adults, we need to struggle to move beyond these roles and provide support for each other rather than antagonizing each other.

Children of all ages, including adults, may imagine that they caused the problem and made Mom or Dad sick. This is called "magical thinking" and it is common among children. A young boy may reason that if he hadn't yelled at Mommy, then she would have been all right. Or a teenager may believe that if she had gotten better grades, Dad would have been all right.

NOT EVEN THE BEST CAREGIVERS ARE PERFECT

It's virtually inevitable that you will make mistakes. Don't condemn yourself and presume all is lost! In most cases, you can regroup and try a more effective tactic next time. I remember describing an incident to Jane's former psychiatrist, who immediately told me that I had erred and I should have done such and such, in a chiding voice.

Although usually respectful of doctors, I burst out in frustration, "Hey! I'm doing the best I can!" She apologized.

My point is that it's easy to be a Monday morning quarterback, but when you're in the midst of serious conflict, sometimes you'll do the wrong thing. You might yell when you should be understanding, be quiet when you should be supportive, and so forth. But we can learn from our errors.

Learn to Expect Less. . . . But Expect Enough

It's understandable that you'll want to rush the ill person back to health as quickly as possible. After all, you love this person! When a psychologist told me that my daughter had a "chemical imbalance" in her brain, I naively asked, "Well, what's the chemical?" I thought that maybe she needed extra zinc or iodine or some other substance in which she was deficient. Take a few vitamin supplements, solve the problem. Let's rush out and buy that missing "chemical." But most mental illnesses are difficult to diagnose and may also be difficult to treat. You need to learn not to expect a quick fix.

On the other hand, be sure to treat the mentally ill person as a person and offer him every chance to perform achievable tasks. Especially after a stay in a psychiatric hospital, everyone in the family is usually walking on eggshells and being overprotective. Of course you should not expect your relative to immediately return to a high functioning level. But it's also important not to discourage your relative's efforts to try. You may be able to start with relatively simple tasks, and work up to harder ones.

Richard Keefe, Ph.D., an assistant professor of psychiatry at Mt. Sinai Hospital in New York, has extensive experience helping patients with schizophrenia. Keefe, author of *Understanding Schizophrenia: A Guide to the New Research on Causes and Treatment* (Free Press, 1994), says that often caregivers blame themselves for the illness and that leads them to expect too little—or too much—of the ill person.

Be encouraging without being intrusive and give the person room to relax. Says Dr. Gary Mosher, a psychiatrist at Circles of Care in Merritt Island, Florida, "You need to create an atmosphere where your relative can function to the highest level they're capable of. You don't want to coddle them too much and you don't want to make it so difficult that their lives are so stressful that they relapse. There's a fine line and it's different for each individual."

Don't Tolerate the Intolerable

One mistake many caregivers make is in being too accommodating to the ill person, essentially letting the person do whatever he wishes no matter how much trouble it causes the family. "Families need to get information about whether a behavior is part of an illness or is a secondary kind of behavior," says Lenane. "Even if it's part of the illness, how can you work to decrease that kind of behavior? There are almost no children [or adults] who can't learn limits on their behavior. Instead, what there are a lot of is families who don't place limits on behavior, and that's an enormously unhelpful thing to do because we don't care for mentally ill people well if we tolerate things that society won't tolerate."

Learn to Cope

Nancy Herman, Ph.D., a sociologist and researcher at the Central Michigan University in Mount Pleasant, Michigan, says that according to her research, the best copers were the ones who worked together. Families all pitched in. They also took it upon themselves to educate themselves about the mental illness. They sought social support or started their own support group. The worst copers "were almost diametrically opposite. They were bickering. They never wanted to talk about it, and they didn't have good communication skills to talk about problems. They were also embittered and felt like now the person was back in the house, they couldn't do anything."

You're never going to like the fact that your family member is mentally ill. Simply protesting that the illness is not fair is not helpful to anyone. Life becomes so much easier when you can begin to accept the fact that a loved one is mentally ill and move on from there.

Retain Your Sense of Humor

Don't tease or hurt the feelings of your ill relative. Having said that, it's important to know that retaining (or regaining) your sense of humor can help a lot. For example, the mother of an ill adult who periodically roamed from state to state (to her great distress) told her supportive relatives that she didn't need planes or overnight service deliveries to get packages places—all she had to do was give it to B.! He could be in New Hampshire one day and Ohio the next.

One woman with schizophrenia went to a Halloween party dressed as a Cogentin tablet, a medication to counteract side effects in antipsychotic medications.

After my daughter's voices went away, the ones that told her in the supermarket that people didn't like her and thought she was ugly, I told the doctor that I was really glad those nasty people who were mean to Jane had stopped hanging around the supermarket. Irony helps.

Humor may also help your ill relative, but remember that many people with NBD are very sensitive and may not grasp sophisticated or witty jokes. Some studies of ill people before and after psychiatric hospitalization revealed a drop of more than 10 IQ points. Also the ill person is often bombarded with internal stimuli and cannot focus on jokes—they can't "get it."

Set Boundaries and Rules

Accepting that mentally ill people sometimes (not always) behave irrationally does not mean that you should allow the person to behave in whatever manner she chooses. Each family must set their own rules and boundaries of acceptable behavior. For example, many families have made a rule that their mentally ill adult children may live with them *if* they continue to take medication. (Refusal to take medication is a common problem discussed in Chapter 8.)

Money is often a problem. The ill person may have none or may have only a disability check. Many mentally ill people have difficulty handling money and some will even give it away. Yet they know that money is tied to independence and adulthood and don't like the idea of someone else being in charge of it. One solution is for someone outside the family to be the payee for the check, although in many families the caregiver is the payee.

Social relationships are important to people of all ages but often mentally ill people either isolate themselves or associate with people the caregiver may disapprove of. It's a constant tightrope walk to help your relative be as independent as possible while still being protective.

Don't Attribute Everything to Mental Illness

One common mistake caregivers make is to believe that every bad mood and every misstep is somehow connected to the mental illness. But everyone has bad days and good days and when your relative acts cranky or irritable, it's not a good idea to say, "What's the matter with you? Haven't you had your medication this morning?" This kind of questioning attributes more power to the medication and to the illness than most people can accept.

Don't Expect Fast Recovery after Hospitalization

Peter Weiden, M.D., director of the schizophrenia program at St. Lukes–Roosevelt Hospital Center in New York City, says that sometimes after a patient is discharged from a psychiatric hospital, family members presume that soon the patient will be all better. But, he says, recovery is more complex.

"It can take up to six months to recover from an acute psychotic episode," says Weiden, who likens the recovery to the patient healing from a broken leg. "Let's say that you broke your leg and they've set the cast. You can walk on it—but the injury is still there."

Weiden says that if the person has schizophrenia, as long as the relative is taking medication and "not doing anything dangerous or problematic—but also not doing much with their lives—don't make an issue of that." Of course, if you feel the person may be slipping into a depression, says Weiden, you should alert the psychiatrist.

Find Patterns, If You Can

As you gain knowledge of what truly distresses your ill family member, you may see emerging patterns. (Although it's also important to state that sometimes there really are no patterns, or at least none that are observable by the average person.) For example, if you observe that your relative becomes stressed out in crowds, then you may try to avoid crowds. Or if your relative can't cope with loud noises and flashing lights, you're probably not going to take her to a video arcade or a busy nightclub.

Finding patterns of behavior that precede psychotic breaks or lesser, but still difficult, problems is particularly useful. Doctors call such a pattern a "prodrome," which refers to symptoms or behaviors that precede a psychotic incident. For example, if your relative gorges on crackers before she goes into a rage, you know when she stocks up on those crackers in the supermarket that you're in for a bumpy ride, emotionally. Knowing this, you can plan ahead, rather than be shocked by what happens.

And what about those times when you get stuck in a situation that upsets your family member? Try to reassure her and try to reassure yourself. For example, when my daughter began panicking in a crowded airport on Labor Day weekend in Washington, D.C., I told her to sit down. I also told her, in a very calm voice, that I understood it was hard to deal with seeing so many people rushing about, but she could get through it. When she began thinking that some people were staring at her, I told her that I didn't notice it myself, but we could move to another area if that would be better. I reassured her that it would be over soon, that we'd be on the plane soon and on the way home. Distracting her in a calm voice did work and can be effective for you, too. Sometimes a gentle and reassuring touch, a pat on the back or on the hand can help.

It's also important to realize that just because a certain situation distresses your relative, this does not mean that you should avoid it yourself. Go by yourself or with a friend to the movies, if you want to see a film that would probably upset your relative. Go shopping with your spouse if your son thinks everyone in the mall is talking about him every time he goes there. Don't make a habit of avoiding all or most of the things that *you* like, in order to help your relative. You will have to make some adjustments, even some sacrifices. But don't give up everything.

We all need to "recharge" our bodies and minds at times. Just like a battery may go dead if you never recharge it, you may become ineffectual and nonfunctional as a caregiver if you neglect yourself.

Consider your own personal needs. You will be a happier person and a better caregiver as well!

State Requests in Terms of What the Family Needs

It's also important to remember that the ill person may not care if you think he is ruining his health by not sleeping enough, or if his room is a mess, or if you are unhappy with other activities. Instead, reframe the way you tell your relative that certain behaviors must change.

Dr. Weiden says that a common mistake is for family members to tell the relative she should do something because it's "for your own good." This is not a good tactic. The person may argue with you over whether it *is* for her own good. Instead, a better idea is to tell the person that the behavior aggravates you or the family and is unacceptable. "Suppose that the parent says 'I don't want you to stay up all night because it bothers me,' rather than telling adults what's better for them. Don't get embroiled in arguments over what is right for the person."

Work on One Problem at a Time

Although mentally ill people often have a normal or even high intelligence level, they may still become confused by an increasing level of demands on them. They may lose skills they previously had. Perhaps the turmoil within is too much to bear and they can only tolerate a limited amount of stress from the environment. As a result, when you decide you want to change or minimize behavior of your relative, you don't go for 100 percent immediately.

Let's say your relative is eating sloppily, not changing his clothes, and refusing to get up at a reasonable time in the morning. It would be a bad idea to suddenly announce that, effective today, your relative *will* eat neatly, *will* change his clothes (and by the way, hang up the ones on the bureau) and *will* get up at 7:00 in the morning. Your relative will most likely respond with confusion and/or anger and you won't accomplish anything. Instead, choose one behavior and try to mold your relative into the appropriate behavior. Praise the person when you "catch" him eating neatly (if that is the chosen behavior). Request calmly and clearly, in simple sentences, that he be more careful when the sloppiness continues.

And do understand that there will be relapses, no matter how effective you are at helping your relative to achieve some normalcy. Everyone spills or breaks things sometimes. Be careful not to attribute all accidents or misbehavior to the mental illness.

Recognizing Real Problems

It's also very important to realize that when your relative tells you about a serious problem, you should not dismiss it out of hand as part of their illness (unless it is something like space aliens landing in your backyard; that is pretty unlikely). Just because a person is mentally ill doesn't mean they imagine everything they tell you. For example, one woman's adult daughter complained to her that her therapist was sexually harassing her. At first, the mother presumed the daughter was just imagining the whole thing, or maybe she had taken some words out of context.

"But by the third visit, I started to get alarmed," she said. "She said he was saying things like, 'I'd like to see your breasts,' and 'I wonder what you look like down there.'" The mother encouraged her daughter to go before a board at this clinic and tell them what happened. An investigation did reveal that this therapist was sexually harassing females and he was fired.

Keep in mind that this is also true with medical problems. Your relative is just as prone to become physically ill as a person without a neurobiological disorder.

Helping the Mentally Ill Person Cope with the Illness

No matter how sick they are, most mentally ill people know that something is really wrong and they may be aware that they are mentally ill. It's okay to tell them that they have some problems, and in fact, it's better to tell the truth than to lie or to ignore the problem altogether.

If they ask you when they will get better or *if* they will get better, you can honestly answer that you do not know but that you are doing everything possible to make it happen. When your relative asks you if he or she will someday marry and have children, it's far better to answer honestly that you don't know than to smile brightly and say, "Of course!" and then retreat to your room to cry.

It is sad and it is hard to be mentally ill and it is not fair. It's not fair to the mentally ill person and it's not fair to the caregiver. Sometimes your ill relative may realize even before you do that this is a long-term problem, but may be afraid to tell you how severe it is or how troubling it is. The person doesn't want to hurt you. Or the person may lash out at you and blame you for everything and anything.

One woman tried very hard to avoid doing the things that upset her spouse, who suffered from explosive rages. But the problem was, she never knew what would set him off. What made him angry last week didn't matter this week. She learned to accept that the rages came from within him and had no relationship to what she did. She was just there when they happened, a ready target for verbal abuse. When she decided that he was the sick person and it wasn't her fault, the situation improved. His rages still occurred—but they didn't bother her as much.

Children can also take advantage of you, whether they are healthy or mentally ill. In fact, says Lenane, "Sometimes I think mental illness gets undue weight. One of the things that's really really important is that if you have a child who has a handicap, it's not going to help that child at all if you add another handicap to it." What does she mean by this? Lenane goes on to say,

> The other handicap can be parents who are so overprotective that the child has no room to grow or parents who make such concessions for the child because of the first handicap that they raise a kid who expects everyone else to make all these accommodations. The hard truth is that the outside world will *not* make the same accommodations to your child's mental illness as you will. I have seen some very psychiatrically ill children who behaved well in public situations. They said please and thank you and they knew that if they were angry, that they needed to deal with their anger.

You feel sorry for Billy because he has a mental illness and he really wants that toy. But his behavior has been awful today and you told him that unless he sat quietly for ten minutes (assuming that such behavior is possible, albeit hard, for him), you would not buy him anything at the store. So don't buy the toy! It's not your fault that the child is ill and you can't make him well by lavishing him with toys, just as you couldn't take Billy's illness away with toys and treats if it were leukemia or cancer—you can't somehow make it better by overindulging him. The same is true in dealing with mentally ill adults.

4

EDUCATING YOURSELF, IDENTIFYING HELP, AND SEEKING SUPPORT

When you are providing caregiving for a person with a neuro-biological disorder, understand that you will need to educate yourself, you will need professional help, and you will need support from others.

Begin by gathering information about the person's illness. Read books and articles, ask the psychiatrist or therapist to recommend information sources, and talk to people at support groups for families of the mentally ill. (See Appendixes E and F for lists of support groups nationwide.)

In most cases, with a little effort you can find people to talk to over the phone or even through online computer groups. For example, America Online offers a forum for people interested in information on topics related to caregiving, managed by NAMI members. This section also includes valuable topics in a computerized library, which you can download onto your own disks. You can also communicate with others online; for example, on CompuServe, the "Mental Health" section of the MedSIG forum is an area where a wide variety of neurobiological disorders are discussed. A section primarily used by mental health professionals, members have also been very helpful to laypeople with questions.

But you need not be a techno-wizard to find support—there are many groups nationwide that meet on a regular basis, in your city or nearby.

EDUCATE YOURSELF ABOUT
THE ILLNESS

One study found that the more educated people are about mental illness, the less they are affected by the stress associated with it. Check your library and bookstore for books you can read on mental illness in general and the diagnosed condition of the person you care for in particular. And don't forget: If your local library does not have a particular book you need, the reference librarian may be able to order it for you through Interlibrary Loan.

Do read books and articles critically, and understand that many books still tend to bash families—particularly mothers—for causing people to be mentally ill. Know that this theory has been discounted today. If you find an article or book that is too difficult to understand, write down the words or phrases that confuse you and see if they are in the dictionary. If you can't find them, the next time you take your relative to the psychiatrist or therapist, ask what these words mean.

Don't expect to become as adept as a psychiatrist or therapist yourself, but do understand that there is a wealth of accessible information describing mental illness. (And you may find that you do become more knowledgeable about your relative's problem than are many therapists!)

Sometimes you will identify contradictory information because mental health professionals (and authors) do not always agree on various issues. "There is conflicting information and it is hard to sort it out," says Gary Mosher, M.D., a child psychiatrist based on Merritt Island, who deals with serious mental illness. Mosher continues,

The fact is that as smart and as advanced as we think we are, there are still a lot of things that we don't know. And there are treatments that work on some people that don't work on other people. People are very complicated beings and we like to reduce things to simple models and simple explanations. Unfortunately, life isn't like that. My advice is to keep an open mind with a healthy bit of skepticism.

GET GOOD PROFESSIONAL HELP

When you are providing care to a mentally ill person, you definitely need the ongoing assistance of a psychiatrist and you may also need psychologists and therapists. This section discusses issues involved with identifying and evaluating someone that your relative likes and can work with as well as someone who will listen to you, consider your opinions, and provide feedback.

It is especially important that you find a psychiatrist whom you, the caregiver, can work with. Some of the people I interviewed said that their mentally ill relatives had told the doctor (or psychologist) terrible and untrue things that the caregivers had allegedly done, and the therapist apparently believed them. You do not want an "us" (the patient and doctor) against "you," (the caregiver) relationship. Nor should you expect the doctor or therapist to tell you everything that is said in private sessions.

Find a Competent Psychiatrist

This is critical because a good doctor may be able to bring your relative up to a high-functioning level while a less capable physician may effect no improvement. Or worse, the treatment ordered by an ineffectual physician could make the ill person even sicker. Why a psychiatrist? Because a psychiatrist is also a medical doctor, with a complete grasp of the workings of the human body. A good doctor will screen your relative for a variety of ailments by taking a careful history and ordering appropriate lab tests.

Psychologists and social workers may also be highly competent in dealing with neuroses, or even in some cases psychoses, but they cannot order medical tests, nor may they prescribe medications. In most cases, medications are essential to the improvement of your mentally ill relative. It's important to note here that psychologists who do work with seriously mentally ill people are usually affiliated with or work closely with a psychiatrist. So it is possible to work with a good psychologist in conjunction with a good psychiatrist.

You may feel ill-prepared to choose a doctor. Said one parent, "At first, it was too scary for me to think there might be significant differences between doctors. I felt like that saddled us with a lot of judgments where we had no experience." It is frightening to consider evaluating a physician, especially if you've always presumed that all medical doctors who are licensed are therefore inherently qualified. It may well be a new idea to think like a "consumer" when it comes to consulting a psychiatrist. But it's an important and valuable mindset change, and one that can save you and your relative many problems later on.

As the caregiver, you will probably have to advocate for your relative at various points. You really cannot be a shrinking violet if you are seeking the best possible service! It's wonderful to have a competent and caring psychiatrist who is on "your side" in battles that may occur with your insurance company, the school system, the mental health system, or the other systems you'll find yourself involved with. So start from that viewpoint—that an excellent, albeit not flawless, doctor is essential.

So how do you get started? Here are some practical tips, as well as a discussion of situations in which neither you nor your relative has a choice about your relative's psychiatrist For example, if the ill person is hospitalized in a psychiatric facility, he may be assigned a doctor, particularly if this is the first hospitalization and the first acknowledgment of psychosis.

Get Referrals from Other Doctors

Ask your primary care physician, pediatrician and any other doctors you know and trust if they can recommend a good psychiatrist. Who would they go to if a family member were suffering from major depression or some other psychiatric illness? Why? Write down all these names.

Obtain Other Referrals

Contact leaders of local support groups such as local chapters of the National Alliance for the Mentally Ill. Describe the problem briefly and ask them if they know of any good psychiatrists in your area. Ask your friends and relatives if they know of a good doctor who is experienced in treating serious mental illness. In some cases, your co-workers may be able to recommend someone.

Keep in mind that in the era of managed care, your health insurance may preclude psychiatric coverage altogether or may specify certain doctors that the mentally ill patient must see.

Check Out Medical Schools

If you're fortunate enough to live near a medical school, call the psychiatry department there and ask if there is anyone there your relative may see. You may be able to find someone with research expertise as well as a rapt fascination with your relative's ailment.

You should also ask the psychiatrists or nurses at the nearest medical school if they know of any psychiatrists in your area with a particular interest in serious mental illness. Don't assume, however, that they will be able to make recommendations. Remember to emphasize that the person is seriously mentally ill. Many psychiatrists—and definitely many psychologists—concentrate on the "worried well," who are facing problems of daily living but are far from mentally ill. They do not wish to treat chronically ill people who may be difficult patients.

What If You Have "Managed Care"?

Many employers continue to separate coverage for all mental health services from medical coverage, despite the fact that most physicians acknowledge that mental illnesses are medically based. Still, there is usually a provision for "out of network" coverage if the doctor you choose is not on their main list of providers. If the physician you locate and wish to consult with is not in your "network" but is the best in your area, then it's usually worth the extra money to get the best treatment possible. Of course, you should also write letters every six months or so to the head of your insurance company, asking them to add this particular doctor to your group. Before lobbying your insurance company, ask the physician whether he or she wishes to be added; some physicians prefer not to be affiliated with any one group or plan.

Interview the Psychiatrist

Many of us have been raised to think of the doctor as "God" and to believe that whatever the doctor says must be true. Instead, you need to have a very proactive attitude in seeking out a mental health professional for your relative, because this relationship will be important not only to the mentally ill person but also to your family. You must overcome your subservient attitude toward doctors (which most people still have) in order to effectively evaluate this person. Of course, you should be polite and respectful, but do understand that your relative is a consumer and the doctor is a provider of health care. These services are being paid for, if not by you, then by somebody else.

Understand that it may be difficult or impossible to find a physician who meets every criterion you've set and realize that doctors are human. Most importantly, does the doctor seem interested in helping your relative and does he or she appear competent and comfortable? Is this a person you feel you can trust? Often, your own gut-level response is your best guide for evaluating a doctor.

Your relative may need therapy in addition to medication and periodic medication checkups. Sometimes the psychiatrist will also provide therapy to the ill person and sometimes a psychologist or social worker will provide therapy. There are also family therapists who attempt to assist the entire family in dealing with the mental illness. It's important for your family to develop criteria regarding what you seek in a therapist. Your relative will almost certainly have more than one therapist over the course of her illness because there is often a high rate of turnover, and therapists who are here this year may not be here next year. This problem is accentuated in psychiatric hospitals, where staff turnover may be great, possibly because of the stresses of the workplace.

Experts emphasize the importance of continuity of mental health care for a person with a neurobiological disorder. The ill person needs to be able to rely on having the same counselor as long as possible. But changes are virtually inevitable, and there is nothing that you can do about this except regroup and assist your relative in locating another good therapist.

Keep in mind that psychiatrists and therapists are humans and are affected by their own backgrounds and training orientations as well as by the day-to-day stresses of life. They are not infallible although their help can be invaluable. Regard them as consultants.

Following are some basic guidelines to use in your evaluation: Try to talk to the doctor or therapist by yourself first. Marge Lenane, a Licensed Clinical Social Worker (LCSW) and Project Coordinator of the Childhood Onset of Schizophrenia project at the National Institute for Mental Health in Bethesda, Maryland, recommends that caregivers talk to psychiatrists alone before deciding on a new doctor, rather than dragging the ill person from one doctor to another. "You don't know for sure whether or not it will be a good connection, but I think it is possible to say, 'We're looking for a new psychiatrist and we've talked to a couple doctors. We're still not 100 percent sure but we think this person might be a good match.'" She also says that it's possible—and a good idea—to empower the ill person to realize he or she is a consumer, too.

Before your first meeting with the psychiatrist, do the following:

- Write down your questions and concerns prior to the appointment.
- Think about your expectations and goals. Write these down as well. This is a good practice before seeing any physician, because it will help jog your memory and you won't forget particular concerns. Be reasonable: Don't presume the physician will effect a complete and instantaneous cure. It won't happen.

Conducting the Interview

Ask your questions politely and respectfully and avoid a jaded "here we go again" attitude. If you've seen many therapists, this may be difficult for you. Ask important "hard data" and "soft data" questions. Hard data indicates something that can be answered with a "yes" or "no" response or with some fact. Soft data is an opinion.

Listen carefully to the responses you receive. If you don't understand what you are hearing, ask for clarification. One way to do this is to paraphrase in your own words what you think the person has said. Don't worry about seeming stupid. It's more important for you to gather the information you need than to impress anyone.

Here are a few key examples of hard data questions to ask:

- Does the psychiatrist or therapist have experience in treating people with serious mental illnesses? About how many such individuals has he treated during the past year? If the answer is one or two, you should find another doctor or therapist.
- In the case of evaluating a psychiatrist, does he or she use medications?
- How much will visits cost you?
- Does the doctor have hospital privileges at a psychiatric hospital or a hospital with a psychiatric section, and if so, where? If your relative needs to be admitted, you want the doctor to be able to treat him in the hospital.
- If you have an emergency, can you call the doctor or therapist? Do they have an answering service?
- How often will your relative be seen? Weekly, monthly, or more, or less? Will you be able to offer your thoughts to the doctor or therapist, too? Can you see the doctor alone or only with the ill person present—what's the policy? Some doctors and therapists don't wish to talk to family members alone because they fear losing the patient's trust. This is not a good or bad policy. It is just a policy, and you need to decide how you feel about it.
- How long does the doctor or therapist believe the ill person will need therapy? A few weeks, a year, forever?

Ask philosophical, "soft data" questions:

- Find out the doctor's attitude toward medication. Does the doctor or therapist believe medication can help mentally ill people? If so, in the case of the physician, what medications has he usually tried on persons with your relative's problem? What if the medication doesn't work?
- Find out whether you will have a collaborative relationship with this person. Do this by asking if the doctor will share information with you, and what kind of information. You will need basic information on medications, diagnoses, and common symptoms so you can provide proper caregiving. For example, if your relative suddenly feels very anxious and upset, is this a common reaction that will go away or is this something that you or your relative should report to the doctor immediately? If the doctor fails to share this information, or if you can't communicate, you are basically flying blind.

- About what level of wellness can your relative hope to attain? One physician told me that when his son became ill and needed psychiatric help, he took him to a psychiatrist who recommended a long-term, incredibly expensive program. "It would have broken us financially," he said. He asked the consumer question: "What are we going to get for this? What is the probability that this is going to work?" When he learned that the probability was practically zero because the psychiatrist felt the illness was so "intractable," this father moved on and found another psychiatrist who felt he could help. It made no sense to consult with a physician who recommended expensive therapy but felt that it would render little if any benefit.

- Does the physician try to learn about the latest medications? New medications are being introduced all the time. If the doctor tells you that he or she sticks with the tried and true, with what's been used in the practice for the last five or ten years, it could be a bad sign. Your relative might be deprived of new and very effective medications if you use this doctor.

- Observe the interaction between your relative and the doctor. Is your relative fairly comfortable? Does the doctor (or therapist) seem to understand and empathize with the ill person? Neurobiologically disordered people do best with mental health providers who are warm and compassionate. Keep in mind that because your relative is ill, she may not be very enthusiastic or even nice to the doctor. But do you think that, over time, this doctor may help because he appears to be sincere and caring? Use your own judgment.

- If you have already engaged another mental health professional (for example, a psychologist), ask the doctor if she has ever worked with this person, and observe her body language and level of enthusiasm. This is important information because you need to be sure your mental health professionals agree with one another. For example, if you have a doctor who believes in medication but a psychologist or social worker working with your relative who thinks psychiatric medications are bad, you and your ill relative could become caught in a stressful and confusing battle of wills. As much as possible, seek out providers who have basic agreements on key issues.

  "How willing is the doctor to be in liaison with the other parts of the care that may need to be provided? You're seeking a partner in what may be a long-term journey. You need to be comfortable with this person's willingness to engage you and your spouse as helpers rather than seeing you as bill payers," says Laurie Flynn, executive director of NAMI.

- If your relative is a minor child, does the doctor have any experience in working with the school system? If not, is he willing to learn? The school environment can have a profound effect on the child's recoveries—and relapses.

- What is the doctor or therapist's basic philosophy about mental illness? Does she believe that there is hope for recovery when a person is severely mentally ill? The wrong answer to the hope question is "no." New medications are being developed all the time, as are other medical advances and treatments. If your doctor thinks the situation is hopeless, how can she truly be actively involved with treatment?

- Ask the doctor what she feels her primary role is regarding medication and therapy. For example, does she perceive herself as the one who should concentrate on monitoring or changing medications but not the one who will provide ongoing support in terms of psychotherapy? Does she feel it's better for therapy to be conducted by a psychologist or therapist rather than by the physician? In some cases, psychiatrists will assume the dual roles of providing medication and counseling; in other cases, the doctor sees her role as primarily one of monitoring medication. Find out. Ask.

Questions to Ask Yourself Later

Part of your evaluation should be based on your own observations after the interview. Ask yourself these questions:

- Did the mental health professional seem to understand and empathize with *you*? Were you basically comfortable with him and did you feel you could trust him with the care of your relative?

- Do you feel you can form a sort of partnership or team with this doctor or therapist? What do your gut-level feelings tell you?

- Did the psychiatrist or therapist seem rational? If he concentrates on counseling people who were abducted by aliens or healing people with past life regression therapy, he's probably not the right doctor for your relative. Yes, there are such doctors, complete with medical degrees. Avoid them.

• What does your relative say about the doctor or therapist, now that you are not in the office? Does he feel positive or neutral?

Consider the Patient's Desires

When evaluating a mental health professional, keep in mind your relative's preferences in a therapist or psychiatrist whenever possible. For example, would she prefer a female doctor? Or would he like a younger or more mature therapist? If your relative does not volunteer this information, ask. A person will do much better with a therapist he likes.

Orientations of Therapists

One major problem in identifying a good psychologist or therapist is that there are a mind-boggling array of orientations. One psychologist said he quit counting at 450. There are several broad orientations, including psychoanalysis, cognitive therapy, and insight therapy (explained below). And there are many others, for example, therapists who concentrate on play therapy.

PSYCHOANALYSIS

You've probably heard of the psychoanalytic view of therapy, now abandoned by many psychiatrists, which views what happened in a person's childhood as pivotal to understanding where that person is now. The individual is expected to improve by gaining understanding of past experiences and traumas and how they affected him; unfortunately, many seriously mentally ill people lack such insight. In addition, neurobiological disorders are not caused by the childhood environment. Thus, psychoanalysis really cannot work for most seriously mentally ill individuals.

One key problem with psychoanalysis is that it fails to acknowledge the biological elements and brain disturbances that characterize serious mental illness. Even Dr. Sigmund Freud, who created the concept of psychoanalysis, was reluctant to treat severely mentally ill people because he doubted that psychoanalysis would be effective. Ask the physician's or therapist's opinion of Freud and psychoanalysis. If this is his or her primary form of treatment, move on.

INSIGHT THERAPY

The major premise of insight therapy is that once patients can understand why they do what they do, they can change their own behavior. As mentioned earlier, the mentally ill person may have a serious insight deficit; thus, this technique probably will not work.

COGNITIVE THERAPY

Cognitive therapists concentrate on helping a person change their thoughts and behavior. Many mentally ill people find it difficult, if not impossible, to change their thoughts. They may be able to change their behavior, however, with the help of a very patient therapist. This is probably the only form of therapy that might help your relative—other than medications. This form of therapy may work especially well with people who suffer from obsessive–compulsive disorder (OCD).

When you meet a therapist, be sure to ask what basic orientation he believes in. He may name a therapy that is a subset of one of those described above. Try to find out which overall category the therapist's orientation can be categorized under. Ask the therapist to explain what his or her orientation is in layperson's terms. For example, one psychiatrist who told me that he concentrates on the psychoanalytic technique actually uses a lot of behavior modification and other techniques. He is probably not unusual in this respect. In the end, it's less important to understand what the overall name of the therapist's orientation is than it is to understand how he proposes to reach the goal of wellness—or at least more wellness than the ill person has right now.

Members of the Clergy as "Therapists"

While members of the clergy receive counseling training in college, the emphasis of their training is on the problems of life rather than on severe mental illness. Since they don't concentrate on providing therapy to very ill people, they may not do an effective job. They may not keep up with the latest research and they may have little or no experience. This is especially true in the area of counseling people with serious mental illnesses, where they may not be licensed or competent to provide treatment, and could cause actual damage to the ill person.

Prayer, however, is one area where religious leaders are usually highly competent and they may be able to provide great comfort and solace to the ill person. Families, too, can gain comfort from prayer. When our entire congregation prayed for my daughter, Jane, at the sincere appeal of our minister, my husband and I found it deeply moving and stress-dissolving. Of course, you may not have a religious orientation or value religious beliefs, but if you do, your religious beliefs and rituals may help you during times of crisis.

Family Therapy

What about family therapy? Many mental health professionals view family therapy as important and feel that those families who receive family therapy are more successful caregivers for their mentally ill relatives than those who don't receive such therapy. Others see family therapy as an indication that mental health professionals still want to bash and blame families. My opinion is that success is heavily dependent on the therapist's competence and general orientation toward the family. Still, it is probably difficult to do family therapy without regarding the family as something that needs to be "fixed."

Family therapy can be a controversial issue. Often, families are highly pressured to include all family members, including the youngest preschool children. (Try to pay attention to a therapy session when your three-year-old is running loose in a small room.) You may also be given the impression that you *must* attend family therapy for your relative to receive help. You may be told repeatedly that you yourself need therapy. The underlying presumption is that the family needs therapy because it must have made the person sick. Fix the family, fix the "identified patient" (the ill relative).

Ideally, families receive therapeutic help in dealing with everyday living problems that they're experiencing with the ill member or assistance in dealing with a current crisis. In the real world, this may not happen; instead, the therapist may decide to concentrate on the "dysfunctional" family. This can be a waste of time for all, or even a disastrous experience.

Said Kenneth G. Terkelsen, M.D., in the 1983 issue of *Family*

Process, "When either therapist or family harbors the belief that schizophrenia is caused by personal experience with family members, therapeutic misalliance is bound to follow." Instead, Terkelsen supported a collaborative relationship. He feels that there are two primary problems with blaming the family for the illness. First, the family might reject the physician in order to protect themselves. Second, the family might internalize the blame and then try to fix the problem. Terkelsen also bemoans his own former treatment of relatives as the problem. "All in all," he says, "my encounters with parents felt like a series of careful negotiations with kidnappers for the release of the hostage."

Another important point is that such counselors often fail to consider that the family may appear "dysfunctional" because they are overcome and overwhelmed with emotional stress resulting from their relative's mental illness. Life is not a one-sided situation, in which the family is solely acting on the ill person and receiving no feedback. It's a constant and dynamic process in every family and more difficult when a member is mentally ill.

If you believe that family therapy is worth investigating, work hard to find a nonblaming therapist with a positive attitude, one who will try to help you find practical solutions and cope with current issues. Also, read Chapter 6, which discusses how you can hold your own family meetings.

Changing Psychiatrists or Therapists

You may be fortunate enough to select the "right" doctor immediately and develop a good long-term relationship. Or you may have signed your relative into a psychiatric facility at a crisis point and been assigned a hospital psychiatrist, possibly one you or your relative dislikes. Although you may not be able to change physicians during the hospitalization, you can find a new doctor afterwards. Do realize that psychiatrists retire, leave the area, or change their interests, so even if you are very happy with your doctor, you may well need to make a change at some point.

One rule of thumb: If the ill person has shown no improvement whatsoever in six months or more, it's time to think about changing doctors. Also, if the physician offers you no hope, you should also consider changing doctors. Your paramount concern should be the best interests of the person in your care. This doesn't mean that you should expect the doctor to paint a rosy and unrealistic picture for you and assure you that everything will be fine. But with today's medical advances and medications, any physician who says that a mentally ill person will never get better is not sufficiently knowledgeable, nor does this person have the right attitude to provide good care for your relative.

You may also wish to change doctors or therapists if you find that a new therapist (or doctor) does not get along with another person who is assisting your relative. For example, if the psychiatrist seems contemptuous of or dislikes your new therapist, you should seriously consider making a change—of either the doctor or the therapist.

Confidentiality

As discussed earlier, issues of confidentiality can be a problem for caregivers because mental health professionals, fearing lawsuits or reprisals from their professional association, may refuse to provide information on medications, treatment, prognosis, and other issues involving adults who are mentally ill. The National Alliance for the Mentally Ill publishes a booklet on confidentiality, authored by Kayla F. Bernheim, Ph.D., entitled *Patient Confidentiality and You*. This booklet offers valuable suggestions on how to deal with this issue. These suggestions include the following:

- If one person in the mental health facility denies you information, try someone else. Look for the most caring and supportive person.
- Consider changing doctors or therapists. If the psychiatrist or therapist absolutely refuses to give you important information, it may be time for a change. If you're paying the bill, it's generally easier to make the change. If not, you may be able to convince your relative to move on to a different mental health professional.
- Educate the staff member. Talk about your relative's needs and how you can't offer good care without knowing such things as side effects of medications. Remember, however, that you should not ask for details of what is discussed in therapy sessions. If this doesn't work, go up the chain of command, talking to this person's boss, and her boss, and so on. Tell the hospital

or clinic's board of directors and be sure to tell your support group members.

- Tell the person who is refusing you information that you won't cooperate with any form of treatment requiring information or assistance from you. For example, as painful as it may be, you may refuse to take your relative home after discharge.
- Some people threaten the psychiatrist or hospital with a lawsuit based on the grounds that by failing to provide them with needed information, the institution is committing medical malpractice. Think hard about whether you actually want to pursue this course. It's a good idea to consult with an attorney before you make this threat.

Oversee Your Relative's Case

Once you've chosen which psychiatrist or other mental health professional to deal with and you begin to meet with them and deal with them on a regular basis, it's very important to keep in mind who said what and when and to follow up. Holly Cmiel, a Key West, Florida, mother of adult twins who suffer from manic depression, says, "I made sure that every single person I came in contact with did what they were supposed to do. I followed up on everything, every medication. I talked to doctors constantly."

She adds, "You have to keep track because these people do not. They go home at five o'clock and forget about your child. You don't." Cmiel says she also kept a diary of who she spoke to, what she said to that person, and what was said to her. This came in handy when clinics and hospitals changed staff or lost paperwork. (Please note that I said "when," not "if.") Usually, the caregiver is the first person mental health professionals turn to for information about the sick client, both background information and information about previous diagnoses.

When You Can't Choose the Mental Health Professional

If you haven't dealt with a psychiatrist before and your relative is suddenly hospitalized in a psychiatric facility, there's no time to perform a diligent search for the best doctor—you get whichever doctor is assigned. You may like this person and even wish to continue on with him after your relative is discharged. Or you may feel neutral about the doctors and therapists assigned. Sometimes you will detest this person.

During my daughter's first hospitalization, she was assigned a psychologist who seemed uncaring. When we'd come to see her about our daughter, we were almost sick with worry. We urgently wanted information and assistance on the problem. But she would spend our one-hour sessions taking calls from others, while we sat there fuming. Our one-hour $100 visits sometimes lasted about half an hour. The hourly fee was never reduced to adjust for the minimal time we received.

In retrospect, it is clear that we should have told her we wanted her to ask the front desk to take messages. Or we could have asked for a different therapist. But we were nearly paralyzed with fear and we were tremendously intimidated by the hospital environment. So we didn't. We would not make that mistake today.

You may also live in an area where there are very few psychiatrists or psychologists; thus, your choices are limited. Expand your radius to include more choices. If your relative had cancer or heart disease, wouldn't you travel far, if necessary, to get good help? The same should be true if your relative is mentally ill.

Note: If you do change therapists, the new mental health professional will almost always want to see information about your relative's past history. You and/or your relative will need to sign an authorization to release this information. See Appendix D for an example of such a release form.

When You Are Happy with the Doctor or Therapist

It's a common practice to complain when you are having problems with mental health professionals, and you *should* bring problem areas to their attention in a respectful and clear manner. But what about those times when you feel that the psychiatrist or therapist is doing an excellent job; that this person's work is, in fact, keeping your relative out of the hospital? Although the patient herself may be grateful for the help, she may also be too ill to express her gratitude. So it's up to you. I agree with one parent who suggested writing a letter of appreciation to the person's supervisor. This is a good idea because your letter will definitely be read not only by the supervisor but also by the person you are praising. Well-deserved praise is a good morale booster and the person you are praising will be very pleased and rewarded for good work.

Mental Health Professionals and Families
Need Each Other

Caregivers provide a nurturing and calm environment, if they possibly can, and they truly care about the ill person. They do their best to help the person achieve whatever optimal level of success is possible. They live with the ill person and can see the daily problems that a therapist might miss in a 30-to-60 minute office visit. They can generally tell if the person is getting better or worse and provide important information to the mental health professionals.

Although mental health professionals usually know the general symptoms of a possible relapse (changes in eating, greatly increased activity level, hearing voices, and so on), they probably do not know the individual and specific prodromal reactions (warning signs that precede a relapse) of this particular ill person. For example, the caregiver may have seen in the past that a sudden obsession with a specific idea, food, or object precedes a relapse in their relative, and thus the caregiver can alert the mental health professional to watch out. The caregiver also tries to ensure that the ill person takes medication, although this can be a difficult problem (see Chapter 8).

On the other hand, the caregiver needs the therapist for advice on neurobiological disorders in general and how a particular disorder affects their relative. Caregivers also need advice on medication and how to treat the ill person in general. For example, the therapist may say that this is a good time to either leave the ill person alone or encourage her to activity.

The therapist can also provide specific advice—for example, that you should give the ill person simple instructions. Rather than telling the ill person, "I want you to get up and get dressed and take the dog for a walk down the street. Oh yes, and don't forget to bring in the newspaper and put it on the table. And what do you want for breakfast?" You could say, "Please get dressed. Then take the dog for a walk." For a person who is having trouble with thought processes, the first set of instructions may cause an overload, resulting in inaction or confused action, and probably a lot of frustration for both of you. A good therapist can help ease the way for both of you, advising you about how to change your lifestyle. A good therapist will also tell you that it's important that you *not* give up your life altogether!

The best relationships between caregivers and therapists are collaborative ones, in which they operate as a team. The therapist is the expert on the illness and the family provides much of the actual love and care. It can be a very rewarding relationship. Or it can be a disaster for all concerned, when it doesn't work.

What If *You* Need Therapy

No one knows how many caregivers seek psychiatric or psychological assistance themselves, but the heavy burden they live with undoubtedly causes many to seek help. You may need counseling, antidepressants, or other medications. Or you may just need someone to talk to who understands.

Unfortunately, there are still those mental health professionals who will want to delve into your childhood, past traumas, and so forth, when what you really need is some assistance in coping with the daily strain you live under right now. Make it clear to the mental health provider what you want and for approximately how long—for example, you may not wish to see a psychiatrist once a week or once a month indefinitely; you may have a different time frame in mind. As a result, you may need to negotiate with the therapist. Remember, you are in control, you are paying for this service (or your company is), and if you are not happy, you can walk away from it.

What's important for both you and the psychiatrist (or psychologist, therapist, etc.) to understand is that you are going through a grieving process. You have suffered a great loss—a loss of what your relative could have been; a loss of what you can now achieve because of the time and money you are dedicating to your relative; and a loss of or change in the quality of the relationships that are important to you.

FIND A SUPPORT GROUP

The sad truth is that many families have no idea that support groups exist, usually in their own city or in a neighboring town. "Tell them that's the first thing they should do!" urged one of the caregivers I interviewed. There are general support groups for all families of the mentally ill, such as the National Alliance for the Mentally Ill (NAMI). There are also national organizations that provide information on support groups dealing with specific illnesses such as depression, manic depression, obsessive-compulsive disorder, and other ailments.

Check your local newspaper. Often, these groups send releases to the local newspaper about meeting dates or times. Unfortunately, sometimes they forget to do this. So you should write to the national headquarters of organizations (or call) and ask them if there are any chapters of the organization in your area. (See Appendix E for a listing of nationally based support groups. Many have local chapters in most states.) Also, call NAMI at 800-950-NAMI.

PART TWO

LEARNING TO COPE

I've covered a variety of problems and issues that we caregivers face. Now, how do we cope with them? This section is devoted to answering this question. What has worked for other people may or may not work in your family's case—but it may be worth a try.

5

HOW TO RECOGNIZE AND DEAL WITH SERIOUS PROBLEM SYMPTOMS

Mentally ill people may exhibit a wide range of symptoms, even neurobiologically disordered people with the same diagnosis. But there are some frequently occurring symptoms that can be very disruptive and upsetting to family members, and this chapter covers some of them. Chapter 8 covers behavioral problems that your relative may exhibit, with some coping techniques that may help you.

At first, many of us pretend that everything is fine; that this unusual action by our family member is just a stage, just a blip on the screen; that the person will get over it. Hopefully, soon. Except many times, they don't.

COMMON SYMPTOMS

Your relative may display a broad array of symptoms. Psychiatrists call some of them "positive" symptoms and others "negative symptoms." Positive symptoms refer to acting-out type behaviors, whereas negative symptoms refers to nonaction behaviors such as apathy, withdrawal, and so forth. Families frequently report that they find negative symptoms such as apathy, withdrawal, not speaking, and so forth most disturbing, because they don't know how to react to these symptoms—until they learn from experience and professional advice how to cope.

Flat Affect (Lack of Emotion)

Sometimes the neurobiologically disordered individual doesn't show much emotion (affect) at all, no matter what happens—this is called "flat affect," and it is typical of people with schizophrenia. If you don't know this, you could become tremendously frustrated trying to please the person. Seeing little or no emotion, you feel you have failed. Families report that this nonresponsive behavior is very hard to deal with. Often the ill person withdraws into himself and may spend hours, or even days, in his room. Should you bring in a tray? Should you go and talk to him? What should you do? It takes some thinking and planning to balance what you are feeling and what you can realistically handle and to decide on a course of action. Families agonize over such decisions until they develop a strategy for dealing with such common—and distressing—symptoms of illness.

The ill person may not respond to your sadness or to displays of emotion. He just doesn't seem to care. And maybe he doesn't. It's another element of the illness. It's not your fault and it doesn't mean he's "bad." Relatives may try to "cheer the person up" and go to great lengths to draw him or her out. Apathetic behavior is fairly common among people recently discharged from a hospital and you should give your relative a few weeks to readjust. Of course, if the person appears suicidal, you should not ignore his behavior. But if all he does is sit around, watch television, or basically do nothing, this is okay; he is recuperating, just as others discharged from a medical facility need to recuperate.

Sleep Reversals

Mentally ill people may have a very distorted sense of time or even have "sleep reversal," which means they sleep during the day and are up all night. This might be all right if they were quiet at night—but often they are not.

Have you ever tried to be quiet in the middle of the night? It seems as if every sound you make is magnified tenfold and if there's anything to knock over, well, there's a good chance you will. It's hard for mentally ill people to be quiet at night, too, and often, they don't even try. This is why I strongly recommend that you tell your relative's doctor about sleep reversal problems. The physician may have an idea to help or may prescribe a medication that will help your relative sleep at night and get back on a normal sleeping schedule.

For the sake of your family, try to resolve this problem. You may need to medicate the person during the day (under the direction of a physician) in order to get him or her tired enough to sleep at night. Work closely with the doctor. Alternatively, if you can't adjust the person's sleep patterns, you might try getting him or her earphones to listen to music or television at night. You might also try relocating the person to the other end of your home.

Not Feeling Real

The person may have a sense of unreality and constantly ask you if they are really "here." This may be hard to understand, and if you try to think about it intensely, it can be very frightening. My daughter repeatedly asked me how I knew that I was real. I couldn't tell her how I knew. I just *knew*. When she began recovering from her illness, after taking Clozaril, she said the most valuable thing about the medication was that she knew she was not in outer space. She knew that she was real and that she was here on Planet Earth.

What's important to understand here—and elsewhere in this book—is that these symptoms, as well as auditory or visual hallucinations and other problems, are very real to the ill person. Mentally ill people's senses play tricks on them. Sometimes, they may not know for sure whether these things are real or imagined. They may constantly check with others in the family, in spite of family members' exhausted assurances that no, nobody is following you, nobody is laughing at you, and so on.

If the person asks you, "Is someone following us?" or "Are they laughing at me?" answer honestly. Usually the answer will be *no*! Do not patronize the person or act disgusted by the question. He is truly concerned and fearful. Remember when you were a child and were afraid of monsters under the bed, or in the closet, that might jump out at you if you looked? That fear was real to you and is even more real to the fearful person with a neurobiological disorder. If he doesn't verbalize the fear, but is acting frightened and has revealed a specific fear in the past, you may ask in a kind voice, "Do you have that feeling of being followed?" If the person does not wish to talk about it, do not press.

Hallucinations

It is not only people who suffer from schizophrenia who have hallucinations. Major depression can be accompanied by psychotic symptoms. People who are manic depressive, or suffering from dementia or other mental illnesses can also experience hallucinations. A hallucination occurs when people's senses give them wrong messages. They see people who aren't there or they hear voices when no one is speaking. Sometimes mentally ill people know the voices are inside their minds, but they are voices nonetheless, and ill people hear them as if the words were spoken out loud.

We all hear things sometimes, such as a tune that keeps going through our heads or the angry words someone just said. The difference is that we know no one is really playing music and the distressed person who yelled at us is gone. The person with a neurobiological disease who is hallucinating does not always know this. In some cases, the ill person may smell things that are not there or have crawly tactile sensations when no one is touching them.

Probably the most distressing aspect of these hallucinations for the ill person is they can't be stopped at will. There is no longer any volitional control, and no matter how hard the person strains to make them go away, it doesn't work. Medications can be helpful, either enabling the person to gain control or, in some cases, wiping the images or voices out altogether. Some tactics work slightly; for example, the person troubled by auditory hallucinations may listen to loud music to drown out the voices in his head.

These hallucinations are painful for family members to watch. It's tough to accept that you, the caregiver, can't make them go away and can't talk your relative out of them. Try to maintain a calm and positive attitude. Do not argue with the person. The best you can do is tell the person honestly that you really don't hear or see the things they are describing. But because the ill person really does see or hear these things, suggest that it may be the illness and empathize with the person.

Delusions

Delusions are false beliefs that the person is convinced are true. For example, if the person with the neurobiological disorder believes that he has a great new plan for becoming a multimillionaire in three days and this plan is incomprehensible to anyone but him, this is a delusion. If the person thinks the CIA is after her, this is (probably) a delusion. If the person believes that there are encoded messages in the cereal box, sent to him alone, this is a delusion.

Delusions are strongly held and it is difficult or impossible to talk the person out of them. Don't try. Instead, you can tell the person that you don't really see it the same way that she does. You can also sympathize and empathize with the person, particularly with the underlying emotion. For example, if the person believes the secret police are after him, you might state that it's frightening when a person feels threatened. Dr. Peter Weiden, a psychiatrist at St. Luke's–Roosevelt Hospital in New York, advises avoiding direct words such as "you" or "I." Instead, use "a person," "they," or some other general subject. This tactic is especially important when the person is paranoid. Of course, if the delusions are dangerous—for example, that someone should be killed because he is possessed by demons—and it appears that the person will act on these delusions, you must take action to hospitalize the ill person and to protect the person in danger.

Poor Hygiene

A lack of personal hygiene is sometimes a problem, for all ages of people with a neurobiological disorder, although not all mentally ill people refuse to get clean. In fact, some people, such as individuals with obsessive-compulsive disorder, cannot stop washing themselves. If personal hygiene is inadequate, the person will have to be ordered or cajoled to bathe, comb his hair, and perform other grooming tasks, with or without assistance. The person may need to be told to wear clean clothes, and sometimes the caregiver will have to lay out clothes for the next day. One obvious and outward sign of improvement is when the person who was indifferent to personal hygiene starts taking baths and puts on clean clothes without being told to do so.

If your family member refuses to bathe, you can tell the person that your family has rules, one of which is that everyone must bathe every day, brush their teeth, and so on. Some people create check-off charts for these tasks. This may work for you, or you may find it too difficult to keep track of—for example, how do you really know that he brushed his teeth? If the individual's appearance is deteriorating, however, you can see that he is not bathing or she is not brushing her teeth or washing her hair. Continue to emphasize the importance of personal hygiene and don't become angry. Perhaps the person is elderly and afraid of slipping in the tub and it would help if you purchased a special handrail that attaches to the tub, or bath mats or some other device. You could also tell the person you'll check on her in a few minutes to make sure she's okay.

One mother said her mentally ill daughter could never quite figure out menstruation, and she would throw her stained underwear in the closet or stuff it under the bed. This is a frustrating problem. If the woman seems to have a regular menstrual cycle, you could track it yourself and ask her if she needs sanitary napkins. You could also ask her to place her underwear in a specific place every day and then you check it at least every few days.

Lack of Insight

Another problem that many people with neurobiological disorders experience is a serious insight deficit. As a result, they may have great difficulty understanding other people's motives or intentions. For example, if someone in a room is laughing uproariously, the ill person may assume they are laughing at him. If you tell her a joke, she may not "get" it and she may wonder if you are trying to trick her or ridicule her in some way.

Do not assume that the ill person will understand the basic signals that people make to each other by body language or verbal shortcuts. Perhaps their neurocircuitry is overloaded by the disorder or their internal voices are crowding out other stimuli. For whatever reason, it is often hard for people with neurobiological disorders to truly understand what is going on. So you should tell the person, in clear and simple terms, what is happening. Do not, however, talk down to the individual.

Paranoia

The mentally ill person who is suffering from paranoia truly believes that someone is persecuting him. He may even believe that the caregiver is after him or hates him, which is very tough to deal with. Feeling persecuted is not a symptom restricted to people with schizophrenia; for example, people who are manic depressive may also exhibit paranoid symptoms. Paranoia comes in a wide range of intensities. Your relative may think people in the drugstore (or anywhere outside the home and sometimes *in* the home) are talking about him, plotting against him, or laughing at him. Or your relative may believe that people are poisoning her food or even trying to steal her brain. Or she may believe that her brain is still intact, but people are transmitting distressing thoughts.

Individual responses to paranoid delusions vary. For example, if your relative thinks she's being poisoned, she'll refuse to eat the poisoned food. So the mentally ill person may become emaciated and sick from not eating. If this is a predominant delusion, one sign of recovery is when your relative decides that it's okay to eat the food, when in the past she considered it very dangerous. If the refusal to eat continues, hospitalization may become necessary.

Sometimes paranoid people think that others are trying to kill them or harass them. It could be the CIA or the FBI or the KGB. It's not clear *why* these organizations are out to get your relative, but he is quite certain that they are. This is the primary reason why people who suffer from paranoid delusions are afraid of police-type figures. One woman was convinced that people were following her. She could feel their presence. She knew they were there. But when she whirled around to confront them, they were gone!

This certainty is so powerful that you can't talk the person out of it. In addition, the person may believe that you, the caregiver, are in on the "plot" if you persist in dissuading them from these delusions. When the delusional belief extends to you, the caregiver, it really hurts. One woman's adult daughter at first thought her mother was the Virgin Mary. Later, she believed that her mother was a prostitute who was persecuting her. She could tell this by her mother's voice. Such bizarre delusions (false beliefs) and hallucinations (false sensory experiences) are impossible to contradict and, in fact, can be dangerous to the caregiver.

Disorganized Thinking

Mentally ill people may make illogical connections between ideas, connections that make no sense to others. They may read something in the newspaper and think that the reporter is sending them a secret message telling them to do or not do something.

People with disorganized thinking find it hard to get a job and, if they do become employed, to keep a job, particularly when a psychotic break looms ahead. One man decided to start his own business, selling guns to foreign countries. So he left messages on people's doorsteps throughout the city, asking them if they had any guns to sell. This alarmed the local citizenry, who called the police. His business plan made sense to the psychotic man, but not to anyone else.

The person may also speak in nonsensical terms, and experts say you shouldn't even try to understand them. You'll just give yourself a headache. Try to communicate with the person with hand gestures or body language. Sometimes your ill relative will be able to understand you if you write things down. Above all, do not tease or mimic the person.

Bizarre Behavior

You may also have to deal with bizarre behavior. If this behavior occurs in public, it can be very embarrassing. For example, one mother told me about going out to lunch with her daughter, who seemed quiet and subdued. Then a waiter handed the mother a menu and the daughter began screaming at the waiter for sexually propositioning her mother, terrifying the poor waiter, who fled, and horribly embarrassing the mother, who decided she wouldn't take her daughter out to eat anytime soon.

Some psychiatrists suggest that if you are embarrassed by your relative's behavior and feel that you need to explain it to strangers, you can explain it away as a migraine headache or a medication reaction. That is a lie, true, but such an explanation is more acceptable to the passing stranger than being told that your relative is psychotic. You could also state that your relative has a neurobiological disorder. Most people won't know what you mean, but it sounds important.

Perhaps your relative is less vocal, but exhibits actions that distress you. For example, your relative may stare at another person in public, discomfiting them and you. Many caregivers politely tell the ill person to stop or convince her to move away when possible. The problem with this is that she may simply shift her attention and stare at somebody else. A different tactic might be to tell your relative that sometimes people get upset when they are stared at and staring is considered inappropriate. Shift the emphasis to others and keep your explanation simple. Screaming, crying, and laughing uproariously at nothing are behaviors that may occur. There are a wide range of bizarre behaviors and no person exhibits them all. (Thank goodness!)

It's a good idea to keep your relative's feelings in mind. Rather than tell the person, "You are acting crazy again," find a polite and clear way to convey the message that their behavior is not appropriate. One example, cited by Dr. Weiden, is the man who is brought into a facility handcuffed, because he was roaming the streets naked. Rather than chastising him for aberrant behavior, the doctor or therapist (or you) could say, "Some people get upset by naked bodies." That shifts the onus from your relative to other people and is easier for the ill person to accept.

Aggression

Although most neurobiologically disordered people are more likely to be victims than victimizers, they may exhibit violent behavior if they feel threatened. Individuals prone to violence are most likely to perform violent acts when they are not taking their medications.

If your relative is in a violent or aggressive state, avoid all confrontations! This is very important, because you could be in physical danger if you argue with the person. Talk to him in a gentle, but not patronizing, voice or don't talk at all if you think anything you say would provoke him. Position yourself so that you have access to the door and you can get out. If your relative responds well to certain people, for example, certain friends or relatives, call them. You may need to call the police. (See Chapter 8 for specific tactics in dealing with 911 and the police. For example, it's important to remain calm. You do *not* want the police to come to your house and be unable to tell whom they are to take custody of!)

Restless Behavior

Sometimes people with neurobiological disorders have trouble sitting still. They may pace, squirm, or be generally nervous. It could be a side effect of the medication they take, or it could be part of their illness, or even part of their personality. (Some people are naturally very active.) You may try encouraging the patient to go for a walk. Go with him if you can. Or you could encourage other forms of exercise such as bike riding, running, or even working out in a gym. Some psychiatric medications cause weight gain, so exercising will be both a positive outlet for your relative and a way to keep her physically fit. You could also learn to accept and live with the restless behavior if nothing you do alters it. Tell the doctor about the problem. Ask for suggestions. He may prescribe a sedative medication or have other ideas.

Inappropriate Sexual Behavior

The public sexual behavior of a mentally ill person can be very embarrassing for the family. In one case, a man masturbated to get rid of demons and nobody could talk him out of it. So when it looked like the demons were coming back, his father or someone else would usher him off to his room. (Fortunately, the demons didn't come to him outside of his home.)

Sometimes people with neurobiological disorders will make sexual overtures or comments to disinterested or repelled people. Because of a lack of insight, they may believe that this is welcome behavior. In some cases, they may believe that God or some inner voice is directing them to pursue this person, a very difficult situation for everyone.

Also keep in mind that not all sexual behavior is unwanted by the ill person, nor is it all bizarre. Many neurobiologically disordered people continue to have a sex drive, although you may wish they did not, because you fear the person may contract HIV or produce an unplanned pregnancy. It's a good idea to make your relative aware of birth control methods and "safe sex." This may be embarrassing when the person with the neurobiological disorder is an adult, because most of us don't like to get involved in the private sexual behavior of others. You don't need to know the details of his or her sex life, but you do need to make the ill person aware of the consequences of failing to use birth control and of the risks that can be involved when psychiatric medication is taken during pregnancy.

If your mentally ill female relative does become pregnant and does not wish to have an abortion (and you cannot force such a choice on her), then you may wish to take custody of the child after birth, with her permission or by taking court action. Your relative may also choose to place the child for adoption, and adoption agencies and attorneys can provide advice and recommend screened people to adopt the child. Sometimes the child will end up in the state foster care system, particularly if your relative is not providing good care. (You may even be the one to report her to social services.) In such a case, you can request permission to care for the child and it will probably be granted; however, social workers may attempt to "reunite" the child with the ill person.

In one case, a woman with schizophrenia was raising her son as a cat. He had no speech and literally crawled around on all fours when social workers took the toddler into custody. He was placed in foster care and the foster parents, through heroic measures, greatly improved the functioning level of the child. They sought to adopt him but an attorney for the birth mother blocked the adoption, stating that it was not the woman's fault that she had schizophrenia and thus she should not be "punished" by losing her child. Fortunately, the birth mother eventually showed more insight than her attorney and she decided to let the adoption go forth.

It's also true that some medications dampen sexual desire, and can cause impotence in males, and this may dismay the ill person, especially if the person has been sexually active in the past. It is also true that the person may be oblivious to a lack of sex drive because other problems seem paramount.

Self-Injury

Self-injury can be an attention-getting device (a very effective one!), or a response to depression or inner voices, or all of the above. The problem is that the ill person may go too far and accidentally kill himself. This is the primary fear of most caregivers. Self-injurious

actions are disconcerting to even the calmest psychiatrist, so it is easy
to imagine how distraught a family member becomes over it. (See
Chapter 8 for information on suicide threats.) One solution that has
worked for some is to have the ill person create a contract with her
therapist or caregiver that she will not self-injure. Also, if she
feels the urge to self-injure, she will first tell someone—a parent, a
friend, or some other person that you agree on in advance. (Try to
think of at least two people.) And she will not do anything until she
has the opportunity to tell one of the people you've agreed should
be told.

The Mentally Ill Person Looks Normal

Although often their appearance and behavior hint at the existence
of a neurobiological disorder, sometimes the mentally ill person looks
just like everyone else. Says Flynn of NAMI, "We almost wish we
could say, 'See, he has a hole in his left cheek, that's how you can
tell.'" She adds that when people see a child on crutches, they don't
assume that he could walk if he wanted to. But often this assumption
is made about mentally ill people, particularly if they look normal.

Studies of autistic children and their parents have revealed that
when the autistic child looks normal or attractive, their parents are
significantly more stressed than parents whose children do not appear normal. In addition, when the children look normal, the parents
are more likely to blame themselves and to be blamed by others for
the child's problem.

It's not only children who may look normal although they suffer
from a mental illness. One woman told me that her husband looked
just like everyone else, although he suffered from extreme mood
swings and had been suicidal and hospitalized several times for manic
depression. "I have friends who periodically say they can't imagine
him acting out that way, and I understand it because he just won't get
in front of people when he's out of control," she said. "I watch him
in social situations and am amazed that this is the person I know. But
I don't necessarily want the rest of the world to see him out of control, so I don't know that I really do want him to look any different."
Still, she is frustrated because she has seen the extreme behavior that
her husband has been able (so far) to conceal from others.

RECOGNIZING SIGNS OF A RELAPSE

With all these symptoms, and with some disappearing and new ones presenting, caring for a mentally ill person can be and usually is an ordeal for the family. Even when most symptoms disappear for a while, they wonder, is this *it*? And it probably is not. As a result, family members must cope with the fact that there are often peaks and valleys in the course of the illness. There are improvements and then relapses, and this may be the usual course of the illness.

The caregiver may anxiously monitor signs of possible relapses and may be hypervigilant, wanting desperately to avoid rehospitalization and the emotional anguish their ill relative (and the caregiver) have suffered in the past. Here are a few signs of possible relapse: hearing voices or hearing the voices more frequently; greatly increased or decreased activity—never sleeping or always sleeping; changes in grooming habits or eating patterns—for example, refusing to take a bath when the person was formerly very clean, refusing to eat meals, or constantly eating when the person ate normally in the past.

There may also be changes in behavior that are specific to the individual and that the family has noted in the past as prodromal symptoms (warning signs). For example, the person may suddenly begin to drink excessive quantities of water or milk. In one case, the prodromal symptom was vomiting. Or the person may self-isolate far more than in the past. It's important for families to share this type of information with clinicians. And it's equally important for clinicians to listen to the family when they report such symptoms. (Sadly, they may not.)

Yet, no matter how vigilant the family is, and even if they could create a chart of the individual's behavior, it still isn't enough. Hospitalization cannot always be avoided, nor should it be. The family must keep in mind that the illness is not their fault and that relapses do not mean they have "failed."

Denial

Many caregivers are frustrated because their mentally ill relatives cannot accept the fact that they are ill. It is too painful for the former family breadwinner or for a once-successful person to acknowledge his or her own limitations. As a result, the person may refuse to take medication or to see a psychiatrist. Or they may take the medication, see some improvement, and decide they are "all better" and quit taking it, and then relapse.

Sometimes the ill person does agree to be hospitalized, but once there, sees all these "sick people" and thinks he doesn't belong there, when, in fact, he may be a lot sicker than the other patients.

6

BALANCE THE NEEDS OF
OTHER FAMILY MEMBERS

Your mentally ill relative is by no means the only person affected by his or her illness, although frequently this fact is ignored or forgotten by mental health professionals. Or worse, it is not even known or acknowledged. Sometimes even family members tend to forget. I'm reminded of an old television advertisement for Al-Anon (an organization for families of alcoholics): "You know what it's doing to him. But do you know what it's doing to you?"

Family members are definitely affected by the ill person, no matter what their ages, their relationship to the ill person, or their attitude or level of understanding of neurobiological disorders. (Although certainly education does help!) Yet, this is the one kind of medical problem that we are not supposed to talk about. When a family member has a serious medical problem such as cancer or severe arthritis, others in the community sympathize with caregivers and their families. Probably the only mental disability for which families receive any sympathy or understanding is Alzheimer's and other forms of dementia. And even they don't get enough understanding.

In one study of families with a schizophrenic spouse compared to families without an ill spouse (the "control group"), the research family's children were significantly less active in extracurricular school activities. They were also far more likely to spend weekends at home as opposed to becoming involved in outside activities.

Who gets shortchanged when one member of the family is mentally ill? Everyone else in the family probably *feels* like they aren't getting enough attention, money, love, and so on. And often, they are right. This chapter talks about the effects of mental illness, both short-term and long-term, on family members.

95

MENTAL ILLNESS AFFECTS THE WHOLE FAMILY

Everyone in a family is affected by the ill person's sickness and the behavior that results from it. Even something as simple as handling chores can cause great resentment. Is the person with the neurobiological disorder forever excused from making her bed or taking the trash out because she's sick? If so, the other siblings will resent it (which is a good reason for continuing to give the ill person tasks to perform as a family member). Some members will feel they can't invite their friends home because the ill person might embarrass them. They may choose to distance themselves altogether. Others struggle to help the person and become frustrated when their efforts don't seem to work.

The ups and downs of mental illness also cause great tension. Something you say today with impunity might cause the ill person to become extremely distraught on another occasion. Often you feel off-balance. Sometimes mental health professionals see the family's distress over mental illness as a clear sign that the family is dysfunctional and made the ill person sick. But what they need to realize is that very often the illness causes the family to become stressed out and even to appear dysfunctional.

In addition, when the ill person does show improvement, families may not get very excited, which could lead some mental health experts to conclude that they just don't care. Usually, that is not the case; it's just that the family has seen improvements in the past and become excited, only to see the person crash to a low functioning level. As a result, the family learns not to become overly excited about an improvement because they know from past experience that it is only transient (unless the improvement does continue for weeks or months). Even when the person with the neurobiological disorder shows considerable improvement from a mentally ill state, the family compares her to the person she was before she got sick, and they know that she will probably not achieve the level of success that she would have without the mental illness. The improvement may accentuate for them what will not happen, rather than what has happened. It's important for caregivers and families to keep in mind that even small improvements *are* victories and that you need to love and appreciate the person as they are now, rather than mourning some ideal that might have been.

Effect on Siblings

If you are the brother or sister of a mentally ill person, and if your sibling became sick when you were children, you probably resented being deprived of attention. If you are younger than the ill person, you may wonder if you have a sort of genetic time bomb ticking away in you. Your brother got "it" when he was 17: Will it happen to you when you reach 17? (Psychiatrists should be able to provide some basic genetic counseling. If they don't, ask!)

Children might also wonder if they somehow caused the illness, just as children often worry that they caused their parents to divorce or caused other "bad" things to happen. Maybe they had a bad thought once and magically, it came true. This is why parents need to reassure children that they did *not* make their sibling sick.

Siblings may also distance themselves from the ill person. One reason may be that they are embarrassed or uncomfortable around the ill person and they don't want to feel guilty by association. They are afraid that their friends will think they might get it. Another reason is that some siblings, especially older children and adults, feel a kind of "survivor guilt." Why are they normal? Was it the luck of the draw? Thus, healthy adult siblings may feel guilty about their own successful careers and marriages, knowing that the ill person will probably never achieve their own level of success.

Says Laurie Flynn of NAMI, "We need to provide information to siblings. People are saying to them things like, 'You're the kid with the crazy brother,' or 'You've got that weird sister who's taking those brain drugs.' It affects the self-esteem and social confidence of the other siblings to constantly explain what's wrong with their behaviorally disordered sibling."

Her solutions are to provide information and to acknowledge the feelings of the non-ill child. "Behaviors that are a problem need to be discussed openly with the siblings, and a kid needs to be allowed to say, 'I can handle only so much,'" says Flynn. "What we want to do is keep a reasonable degree of understanding and communication between the ill sibling and the well sibling because they, too, can provide support and reinforcement and normal feedback to the ill sibling."

Marge Lenane, a Licensed Clinical Social Worker (LCSW) and Project Coordinator of the Childhood Onset of Schizophrenia project at the National Institute for Mental Health in Bethesda, Maryland, agrees that it's very important to talk to the non-ill siblings about their feelings. "A parent might say to the child, 'I don't know if you feel this way, but sometimes I wonder if you're jealous of how much attention Thomas gets. Sometimes I wonder if you get sad and worry about whether or not you're important to me,'" says Lenane.

She adds, "I think when we say various accepting things like that, we give the child permission to say how they feel. They may feel exactly that way or they may feel differently, but if we can convey to the child that we can tolerate and accept their unhappy feelings of pain, they're much more likely to be able to express them to us—which decreases the very feelings that they're talking about of anger, resentment and rage."

Adds Flynn, "I think the healthy sibling of the child who is mentally ill is probably in the most difficult spot of anybody. A great shift of attention goes to the ill person. We really need to watch that this may be sending a very negative message to the well people in the family: If you want to get Mom and Dad's attention, you have to have problems."

Lenane says that even small children should be talked to about their feelings. "Little children can be given answers that are age appropriate and they can also be given the message that you probably have a variety of feelings about this and I would like to hear what they are. For example, you could say, 'Does it bother you when your grandmother comes over and tries to force you to give up your toy to your sick brother? That's not right, Grandma shouldn't do that. Let's talk about that with Grandma next time."

"It's important to really listen to the child, and really say that the child has the right to feelings, whatever they are." Lenane says that sometimes parents find it difficult to realize that well siblings may be suffering.

Effect on Parents

Probably the largest group of caregivers are parents, and they are tremendously affected by caring for a mentally ill child. It happens to parents of all socioeconomic strata. The initial horror and fear are the same, whether you are a cashier at a convenience store or a high-powered executive. Why? Because you love your child and want success and happiness, not pain and suffering, for your child. You want a normal life for your child, whether your aspirations are to see him with a Ph.D. or a high school diploma.

As a result, when your child becomes mentally ill, it hurts. It hurts a lot. You feel like you should be able to fix it. You cared for your child as an infant, you proudly watched him grow, you had so many dreams, and now many have come crashing down. You wish you could take on the pain yourself rather than see your child suffer. But you can't do that. Instead, through acceptance and love, you can help your child, whether he's 14 or she's 40, to attain a level of happiness and competency in life. You adjust your expectations but you don't cut back one bit on the love. And you learn to let go a little, and allow the person to falter a few times.

Sometimes the ill person may be better off living away from you, where he would not be protected as much and might be expected to do more than you require in your own home. Or the ill person may need to live with you and you want her to remain in your home as long as that need continues. If your relative is an adult, it's hard not to treat him as a child when he continues to live with you, particularly if he has a neurobiological disorder. You must learn to give your relative the respect and dignity of an adult, while taking into account his limitations.

It's a delicate tightrope for parents to walk, balancing between holding on and letting go, and you must make continual adjustments as the illness fluctuates. Many parents gain great solace as well as practical advice from joining support groups, where they can share helpful hints and trade stories with others who truly understand.

Effect of an Ill Parent on Adult Children

If your parent becomes mentally ill at age 50 or 60 or older, what about you? Could it happen to you? Adult children face not only the pain of the present but the fear of the future. Obtaining genetic risk information can at least help define some of the odds, although they are by no means definitive, as in "You will get this" or not.

In addition to these internal struggles, adult children usually have their own families to raise and their careers to handle as well. What do we owe our parents? What do we owe our children? And what if both are in a tug of war for our time, love, and attention? This is the terrible conundrum faced by the adult who cares for his or her parent.

(For more information on the role of the adult child caregiver, read Chapter 9.)

What if you are *not* the caregiver for your ill parent? You'll also experience the guilt and fear. You may wonder, was it something I did? Could I have been a better child? A better adult? You need to learn and accept that this illness is independent of your behavior and of any action you ever took, whether you were a model child or the terror of the neighborhood, whether you are a paragon in the community or just an average person. It doesn't matter. The illness wasn't caused by you any more than cancer, heart disease, or diabetes.

FAMILY MEETINGS

One thing we did try, at the suggestion of a psychologist, was holding our own family meetings. We set them up for a certain time (for example, every Friday), and everyone had to attend. Sometimes we had a topic and sometimes we didn't. Sometimes the topic was serious, such as how name calling can be painful (after one of the children had a problem with this), and sometimes it was something fun, such as where we should go on vacation. These meetings worked well for us because my husband and I still maintained our parental roles (which was nearly impossible in family therapy, where the therapist acted as a "parent" and we adults were equal to our own children). Yet, everyone had a chance to express feelings and worries, and to talk about silly events as well.

If you'd like to try family meetings, I would encourage the following:

- Make sure that everyone knows what day and time the meeting will be and knows that they are expected to be there.
- Don't start the meeting until everyone is paying attention. No newspapers or books are allowed, and no television, either. Screen out as many distractions as possible.
- One person will often naturally present as the leader, although you can try varying the leadership from week to week. This person should work to make sure that every family member has a chance to say something. At the same time, don't let anyone (including the leader) dominate the discussion.

- If one member is hanging back, ask that person what he thinks. With this encouragement, he may come forward and offer constructive information.
- Make some ground rules at your first meeting and follow them. One rule we established was that we would not tease or insult each other. (This can be a hard rule for children to follow, especially when it concerns their siblings. Do it anyway.) What I learned was that once the rules become known and clear, other family members will jump in and work to insure that they are being followed.
- Don't assume that you'll make dramatic progress, or any progress, at each meeting. And don't assume that your family members will be in love with this idea, either. The concept takes work and practice. Sometimes you may leave meetings feeling energized and happy because tough issues were resolved. Other times, you may feel like screaming afterwards. But at least feelings were vented and issues addressed.
- Limit the meetings to about an hour. After that time, people of all ages get impatient and nervous. They want to eat, exercise, watch television, or engage in some other activity. Release them after the one hour period, even if you feel that you're having a major breakthrough in your interactions. Only if the whole family agrees to continue should you do so.

7

THE CAREGIVER NEEDS SOME CARING

When You Need Help Yourself

As you struggle to make sense of your relative's illness and to provide the best care that you can, you may find yourself ignoring your own needs. Many caregivers worry so much that they develop health problems. Here are a few common symptoms of caregivers to a mentally ill person.

COMMON PHYSICAL PROBLEMS

Physical Exhaustion

Sometimes caregivers are completely worn out, not just from the daily burden of caregiving, but from additional demands as well. For example, some ill relatives have a day–night reversal, in which they want to sleep all day and stay up all night. This might be okay if they were quiet, but many are fearful and excitable and may continually wake up the caregiver. This is particularly tough if the caregiver is working full-time outside the home.

A kind of bone tiredness is common. As a result, it may not seem worth it to continue with a social life. It's just too hard.

To continue (or to create) a social life for yourself, you have to make a plan. You need to plan not only where to go and what to do but often who will stay with your relative. You know you need someone who is caring and understanding. At the same time, you may feel that you don't want to burden others. The whole effort seems like too much work. So, too many times what you do is stay home.

This is a mistake! It's very important for you to make some sort of outside life for yourself. Force yourself to make plans to go to a club meeting, meet with friends, and engage in positive social activities. Make appointments for these events and keep them. And if you still can't drag yourself to a social event that you would have formerly enjoyed, get a medical checkup to rule out a physical problem.

You may also be suffering from depression, which is treatable with medication. Although depression is usually considered a biologically based illness, the strain of coping with a mentally ill person day after day can cause depression in a person who is prone to it—and possibly in a person who is *not* prone to it. It is very hard to be optimistic and upbeat when your relative is clearly and rapidly deteriorating before your eyes, despite all your best efforts. If you need some professional help, seek it out! You don't have to be psychotic to see a psychiatrist—in fact, most psychiatrists treat nonpsychotic people.

Physical or Mental Illness

Sometimes caregivers develop medical problems due to stress, lack of sleep, and general worry. Experts say that a significant number of caregivers suffer from depression themselves, as a direct result of the caregiving role. Fortunately, medicine can help with this problem.

A related problem is that in your passionate desire to help the mentally ill person, you may end up neglecting your own health. Some health problems may become chronic, such as frequent infections or colds due to being generally "run down." The stress and physical strain of caregiving for a mentally ill person can actually make you sick. It's easy to forget to eat nutritious meals—or to eat at all—when you are worried about your child, spouse, sibling, or parent. Stress and grief can cause a wide variety of physical symptoms, such as diarrhea or constipation, stomach pains, heart palpitations, and a myriad of others.

After her son became ill, Holly Cmiel suffered stress attacks in the physical form of diarrhea, sore throats, rashes, and general aches and pains. "In the beginning, I went to doctors and they could never find anything wrong with me. Then it dawned on me: It always happened when my son was in crisis." Her solution? She told herself, out loud, "This is stress!" This worked for her. Once she identified the problem and acknowledged it, it went away. In one case Cmiel was driving to the doctor's office, covered with a rash that frightened her. She then thought, hey, maybe this is stress again, and tried her out-loud solution. By the time she reached the doctor's office, the rash was completely gone.

On the other hand, don't delay important medical procedures, up to and including needed surgery. You are an important person, too.

OVERCOMING CAREGIVER BURNOUT

Lack of Social Interactions and Emotional Drain

Some studies have reported that the lack of social interactions with others outside the family, with friends and extended family members, was the hardest part for the caregiver. If you can't leave the house for too long, it's hard to have a light-hearted time with your friends, especially if you are worried about what is going on at home.

Don't allow yourself to become a recluse! First, acknowledge the problem and assert your right to have a life apart from the caregiving role. Next, find some activities in which you can participate, if only for an hour or so. And remember that if your relative needs constant care, maybe it would be better if he lived in another place where such care could be provided. At least consider an option such as a group home.

Living with and being the primary caregiver for a mentally ill person of any age can be emotionally, as well as physically, debilitating. In one study, mothers struggled to remain silent when their ill children expressed information they clearly felt was wrong. In one interview, the mother turned to the interviewer, stuck out her tongue, and then held it—to indicate she was "holding her tongue" and purposely not speaking. This was her way of expressing feelings rather than repressing them and consequently becoming resentful.

Fear

When the ill relative (usually a male) becomes violent, it appears that he is more likely to attack a female than a male caregiver. This may be because the female caregiver is often the person who dispenses medication, an area of conflict for many mentally ill people. Or it may be because she is the primary caregiver, the one he is around most of the time, and an obvious target. As a result, in the case of parents, mothers report a significantly higher level of fear than do fathers. (And violence is not limited to mentally ill males; females may also attack a caregiver, although it is generally less likely that this will happen.) If your relative becomes violent, call the police. Do not allow yourself to become a punching bag, and do not accept aggression as a fact of life.

OTHER PROBLEMS

Not only are your physical health and your emotional well-being affected, but as a caregiver, you may face other problems as well.

Financial Problems

In addition to the tremendous emotional toll that serious mental illness takes on families, there are often financial burdens. Many insurance companies provide no, or low, benefits for mental health coverage. Many insurance payers also separate out psychiatric services, including hospitalization in a psychiatric facility, from other medical services and from hospitalization in a general hospital and they provide less coverage for psychiatric services.

In other words, your health insurance may pay for you to have your tonsils removed. But if you are suicidally depressed, well, it probably won't pay for a sufficient hospital stay. So families dig into their savings, sell their homes, do whatever they can to get the help they need. Keep in mind that often the ill adult may be eligible for Social Security disability benefits or Medicaid, which are discussed in Chapter 17. This is an option for your relative, despite past earnings—or no earnings—and without regard to the family's income.

One woman said she refused to sign any agreements to pay the hospitalization bill for her mentally ill adult son, who had been hospitalized without her knowledge. Although she agreed that he did need to be hospitalized, she feared that once she started paying, there would be a never-ending stream of bills and she would probably lose her house and everything she owned. (And she was right.)

The Daily Routine

Sometimes it's the little things that get to you. You've survived all the difficult problems, and then something minor happens and you can't stand it. It's the last straw. This is also true when you live with a person who suffers from a neurobiological disease. When a family member becomes mentally ill, the tasks he or she performed in the family before have to be done by someone else, or not done at all. These could be tasks as major as bringing in the bulk of the family income or as minor as household chores.

Give dishwashing, vacuuming, and other tasks to an already stressed-out family member, and you can have problems—resentment, anger at the sick person, the whole gamut of feelings. But in our society, you're not supposed to be angry at sick people. It's okay to have these feelings! But avoid venting your anger on the ill person, because increased stress can exacerbate psychotic symptoms. Instead, find an outlet for your frustration, whether it's holding your breath and/or counting to ten, vigorously exercising, or reading a book. Identify what works for you.

Lack of Time

Caring for a mentally ill person requires a lot of time, particularly in the early stages when you are trying to figure out what's going on, find a competent psychiatrist, and deal with your immediate and extended family.

"Be sure to tell your readers about how time really gets compressed," says the father of a young adult who is mentally ill. There's time spent driving the person to the doctor and/or the therapist and time spent waiting; time at the pharmacy waiting for medications; time spent talking about the problem; and time spent worrying about it. So much time. Do not allow yourself to fall into this trap of spending virtually all of your time on your ill relative and giving up every activity that you or other family members enjoyed in the past! Allocate time for yourself and don't put yourself last when you budget time. This is a common mistake and one you need to avoid making.

REDISCOVERING YOURSELF

Sometimes we get so wrapped up in fulfilling the needs of the ill person that we have to go back a few years (or more) to remember what we did for fun before our family member became sick. If you don't think this is true in your case, try this mental exercise. It may help you to write down your responses. Think back to when your relative was well (if there was such a time), or when you were not providing caregiving to your relative. Make a list of what you did in your free time. Then try to recall how frequently you participated in those activities back then.

Write down at least three different activities from the past, and more is better. It doesn't matter whether they were socially relevant; they need only be things you enjoyed doing. If reading romance novels was fun for you, write that down. Then write down why you liked to do these things. It was fun, it was physically challenging, it was spiritually uplifting, it was important—whatever reason you want. Now make another list. This is the list of what you do for fun now. Compare your two lists. Is the second list much shorter than the first list? Do you see any patterns? Have you scaled back or given up activities you liked?

Go through your first list again, item by item. Do you think you might like to return to some of those activities? Assuming that you could still physically perform them, make a plan. Get someone to watch your relative, or leave him alone if you can, and go for it! Even if you can't do exactly what you did before, perhaps you can find a variation on the activity. Maybe you loved extensive socializing. Why not invite a friend out for lunch? (And you are not allowed to say more than a few sentences about the ill person during lunch. This is a "getaway" activity.) If you were physically active and are less so now, maybe you could join a health club or start taking walks with a friend or neighbor.

Use your imagination to create a good plan for yourself. And the first thing you must do is throw out phrases such as "I can't" and "I don't have time." If not now, then when? Never say never. And if you need an altruistic reason for all of this, remember that a happy and healthy caregiver is far more effective than a burned-out and miserable one.

8

PROBLEM SITUATIONS AND EFFECTIVE COPING STRATEGIES

There are a variety of problem situations that many families face, regardless of the type of mental illness. Here we'll discuss the most common ones, and what to do to cope with them. Other problems such as substance abuse and criminality are discussed in Chapter 18.

REFUSAL TO TAKE MEDICATION

Mentally ill people stop taking medications for a variety of reasons. Try to find out why your relative is "noncompliant," because if you know the reason, you may be able to counter it. Here are a few reasons:

- They believe they don't need medications anymore. (Or they think that they *never* needed medications.) To counter this, try to find some aspect of the person's life that improved while she was on medication. (See the section in this chapter on "Some Do's and Don'ts.")
- They don't like the side effects that the medications can induce, including drowsiness, tics, and weight gain. Talk to your doctor about this and perhaps a decreased dosage could be arranged or another medication could be ordered to counteract these side

effects. Also, ask the doctor for other suggestions or come up with some yourself or with the help of your relative. For example, if the medication makes the person tired, can it be taken in the evening? Or perhaps another medication can be ordered to counteract this symptom.

Some medications may cause weight gain, which can be distressing to women who pride themselves on their figures. I once talked to a woman who was not mentally ill and mentioned to her that weight gain was one side effect of a psychiatric medication—but the good news was that the medicine was very efficacious. She told me, quite seriously, that she'd rather be mentally ill than gain any weight. Sadly, this type of attitude seems to proliferate in our society and it affects us all, including people with neurobiological disorders. Again, perhaps the physician can offer some suggestions to counteract weight gain. In my daughter's case, when her medication caused her to gain weight, she joined a health club and exercises very actively. This has worked well for her.

- Someone the ill person respects thinks "drugs are bad" and convinces the person that he doesn't need them or that the medications will make him sicker. This is a difficult argument to counter because it is based on some irrational premises. The one thing you should not do is criticize the ill person's friend, because that will usually cause defensiveness. You might try asking the person, if he were ill with pneumonia, would antibiotics be okay? If she had a headache, would a painkiller be okay? Psychiatric medications are designed to resolve symptoms, too. You might also consider talking to the person who is antimedication and explaining why some medications are beneficial and why you hope your relative will take the medicine.

- The medication regimen is too complicated for the ill person. If you don't wish to dispense the medication yourself, you do want your relative to be able to comply. It's important for psychiatrists to try to make the medication schedule as simple and clear as possible. Keep in mind that some medications are available by monthly injection, which is a lot easier to manage than oral medications taken daily.

- A power play is going on between the ill person and the caregiver. He knows if he refuses medication, the caregiver will probably get upset. Or the ill person may try negotiation. "I'll take my medicine if you _____." Whether you wish to go along with this is up to you. If the thing the ill person wants is not such a problem, you may wish to give in. Better, you could start or continue the negotiation yourself by saying, "After you take your medication, I'll give you _____."

- Forgetfulness. In this case, you may be able to link the medication schedule with daily events; for example, meal times or before they go for their evening walk. In addition, you could purchase an inexpensive pill box with pills inserted for each day. Thus, if the person doesn't remember whether he took the medication, he can look and note that, for example, the Wednesday pill(s) is still there. You may also consider injectable long-lasting medications when forgetfulness is a serious problem.

It's also a good idea to realize that noncompliance with a medication regimen is common and is not limited to mentally ill people. (This may help you with your frustration level.) Think about times when you didn't take a medication a doctor prescribed, or you didn't take a full course of it for your own reasons.

As important as it is for mentally ill people to take their medications, we need to understand that they are human and sometimes they don't want to take their medications for a lot of the same reasons that we have not wanted to take medications. This doesn't mean that the ill person's reasons for refusing medication are valid or reasonable or that you should just give in. Taking medications is important because doctors estimate that as many as 40 percent of all psychiatric relapses are attributable to one thing: The person quit taking medication. Keep in mind that forgetting or skipping one or two doses of medication doesn't constitute noncompliance.

Indications of Not Taking Medication

Unless you give the ill person medication yourself and see her actually swallow it, you can't be completely sure that the medication is being taken. Some signs of noncompliance in the case of adults who take their own medications are:

- There are too many pills left in the container. The person received a 30-day supply of the medication and it's a month later, but there are 29 pills in the container.

- The person has no idea what his medication regimen is or what the pills look like or are called.
- The person hasn't been filling prescriptions.
- Symptoms that had disappeared with the medication are back. For example, if the medication made the person calm and she is now very nervous, this may be a sign that she is no longer taking it.

Some Do's and Don'ts

- Don't use the medication as a psychological club. If the person is arguing with you and being altogether difficult, do not say, "You better take your medicine. You sure *need* it." This gives the medication more power than most people can willingly accept. (Even if you may be right, it's okay to think to yourself that the person needs the medication right now, but don't *say* it.)
- Don't administer medication or advise a person to take medication when you are in the middle of an emotional scene. Wait a while, then calmly advise the person that it's time for his medication. Says Dr. Weiden, "If you see your relative is getting hostile or like a bull in a bull fight, back off, drop it. Get help from someone else or hospitalize if necessary, but do not get into a fight. It's too dangerous."
- Find out why the person doesn't want to take the medication. If the medication is causing a physical problem, maybe the doctor can lower the dose or make another suggestion.
- Obtain solidarity in your family about the value of medication. If one person thinks medication is unimportant, or even harmful, the ill person may gravitate toward that "ally" and create a struggle. Conversely, many mentally ill people have reported that the reason they have taken medication is that it is important to other people they care about.
- Educate the ill person on the possible side effects of any new medication. That way, your relative won't panic if any of these side effects occur. Better yet, have the doctor explain the side effects to your relative and you repeat them later. Be sure to underscore that there may be no side effects at all.
- Accentuate the positive reasons for taking medications, in the person's own frame of reference. For example, if the ill person

truly wishes to return to work or school, explain that this medication may make it possible to achieve that goal. Also offer shorter-term reinforcements—maybe the individual is better at playing video games when he takes his medication.

- Offer positive reinforcements. For example, "After you take your medication, we'll be ready to go to the movies."
- Relate your own experiences. Talk about a time when you were on an antibiotic and you quit taking it after a few days, and then you got sick again.
- Don't try to convince the person he should take his medication because it helped him so much before. If you convey the idea that the person is well because of medication, your relative may stubbornly quit taking medication to prove you wrong.
- Don't call the medications "drugs." The word has an extremely negative connotation. Instead, use "medicine" or "medication" or even "meds."
- Don't lie to your relative about the medications and don't sneak them into her orange juice or food. Eventually, she will find out and become distrustful of you, and probably even less likely to take her medication.
- Don't tell your relative that the medications will solve all psychiatric problems. Although many medications have powerful curative effects, we can't really know what will work on one person until it is tried.
- Don't panic if the person flat out refuses to take her medications. Sometimes that happens, no matter how hard you try, plead, and cajole. As previously mentioned, you may be able to request an injectable form of the medication that lasts for a longer term, and your relative may be more willing to comply with that kind of regimen.

Forcing Medication: Outpatient Commitment

With the permission of the court, it is possible to involuntarily commit a person to a psychiatric facility. It is also possible to commit people to outpatient treatment, thus forcing them to take their medication. This is an available option in most states, although the laws regarding this procedure vary.

The mentally ill person may be ordered to go to a clinic or other facility to receive oral medication or an injection of a long-acting medication. In some forms of outpatient commitment, there is a stay placed on inpatient commitment as long as the person complies with obtaining outpatient treatment. If he does not comply, a commitment order will be issued. In other forms of outpatient commitment, there is no plan to hospitalize the person, but the person is ordered to be treated in an outpatient setting.

The conditional release from a hospital is another form of commitment, wherein the person is discharged from the hospital prior to the end of the commitment order but must receive outpatient treatment. The hospital director makes the decision for this type of release, rather than a judge. There are also combination forms of outpatient treatment orders, used primarily in the case of treatment refusals by the patient.

With regard to the outpatient commitments that require judicial approval, "The court must first determine whether or not the person is mentally competent to refuse treatment," says Samuel Jan Brakel, law professor at DePaul University in Chicago and vice president of administration, legal affairs and program development at the Isaac Ray Center. "If it [the court] finds him competent, the refusal must be honored. Only if there is, first, a finding by the court that the person is *not* competent to make treatment decisions can the court even take up the issue of whether medication can be administered over the person's objection."

If the court finds the person not competent to make treatment decisions, then the court has to decide what the person would have done had he been competent. Meaning, would he or would he not have taken the medication? "When there is no evidence to guide the outcome on this substitute judgment inquiry, the court may decide the matter based on the person's 'best medical interest,'" says Brakel. "In most states, this ridiculously unwieldy two-step judicial process must be applied even against persons who have been involuntarily committed to a mental hospital, but who refuse to take their medications."

This means that even if the court ordered the person to be committed to a psychiatric facility, that order alone isn't sufficient to force the person to take medication. Brakel says that in practice, when psychiatrists pursue judicial permission to involuntarily medicate a patient, they usually get it. The problem is time—it may take months for judges to agree with the physician that the patient truly needs the medication and must take it. In that interim, mentally ill people may rapidly deteriorate. Psychiatrists are often reluctant to pursue the issue.

"In other words," Brakel explains, "patients may go untreated or inadequately treated because the providers don't want to fight the matter in court." (And who can necessarily blame them?) Times may be changing slowly. "I think there is some slight movement toward restoring the rights of families and caregivers," Brakel says, referring to a handful of states that are changing their laws in this direction. "I think there has been over the years some substantial slippage in public support of the extreme civil liberties position, and this is beginning to affect the decisions of politicians and judges." Brakel also sees signs of a mood to "assert greater authority over the lives of people who can't manage their mental illness."

He continues, "To legally afford full powers of choice to people who empirically show they can't function autonomously is today being recognized increasingly for the anomaly it is."

How do you know what the law is in your own state? In many cases, you can look up the law in your public library or you can go to the law library at the courthouse and ask the law librarian to help you find the state laws regarding outpatient commitment. It's also a very good idea to consult with support group leaders at the local or statewide level. They should be able to provide you not only with information on state laws but also with practical tips on how to get your relative into one of these programs.

SUICIDE THREATS

There seems to still be a prevailing myth that people who threaten suicide don't really mean it and are just seeking attention. But sometimes they really *do* mean it and this section discusses some indicators that the person is serious about this threat.

Many mentally ill people are at high risk for following through on such a threat and you should heed them. The first few months after a discharge from a psychiatric hospital are a high-risk time for suicide. The mentally ill person may be upset about the psychotic break that occurred, or depressed. Over half of all the people who kill themselves have some form of mental illness. Of those who succeed in killing themselves, about two-thirds communicate their intention to someone beforehand.

In some cases, the person may not wish to kill himself but may instead be under a dangerous delusion—for example, if he jumps off a bridge, he will be unharmed because he has super powers. Try to determine what circumstances seem to affect outbursts of acting on such delusions. Talk to your relative's doctor. And realize that you can never watch a person 100 percent of the time. If the person seems to be (or is) acting out in a very dangerous way, then he is a "danger to himself" and should be hospitalized, voluntarily or involuntarily.

Are Suicide Threats Always Real?

A suicide threat may or may not be "real" in the sense that the person will actually attempt to carry it out, but certainly any threat should be taken seriously. Don't assume that your relative is just trying to get attention or to aggravate you. People who talk about suicide sometimes follow through, particularly if they are mentally ill. People with schizophrenia and major depression are particularly at risk for committing suicide—they are about 100 times more likely to commit suicide than a person in the general population. What if the person is a child—they never commit suicide, do they? Yes, they do. Take it seriously.

Sometimes the ill person will commit suicide after an upswing from a serious depression. He or she may still be depressed, but now has enough energy to accomplish his or her goal. Some high-risk signposts of a person who is truly likely to attempt suicide are:

• The person has tried it before.
• The person has a plan to carry out the suicide.
• The person has the means to carry out the suicide plan; for example, if she says she would kill herself with a gun and guns are available.
• The person has been discharged from a psychiatric hospital within the past few months.
• The person has abused drugs or alcohol. Substance abuse can

cause a serious flareup of psychosis, which could then lead to suicidal tendencies.

• The person does not agree to talk with a therapist or other person if the ill person feels suicidal.

• The person has recently lost a child or a spouse. A child may commit suicide over the death of a family member, or even a pet.

• The person is suddenly exhibiting very different behavior. One high-risk sign is if a depressed person is no longer acting depressed. He may have decided that the correct course for him is suicide and this conviction has made him seem outwardly better.

Some clinical symptoms of the suicide-prone are sleep disturbances, lethargy, apparent depression, self-neglect, and memory-related problems such as a difficulty in concentrating. In one study of 71 depressed people who had committed suicide, it was found that none of the 24 psychotic individuals were receiving sufficient medications. In another 24 cases, the patients were taking no antidepressant medications. It seems clear that a psychopharmacological intervention could have saved at least some of these unhappy people.

PARANOIA OR PHOBIAS

If someone is very frightened or phobic, that fear is real. Don't tell the person the fear is silly or try to talk him out of worrying about it. That doesn't work. It's also important to keep in mind that a person in the throes of a psychotic paranoia is very dangerous and you may be at risk for physical harm. Here are some suggestions Dr. Weiden offers for handling such a situation:

• Stand next to the individual instead of looking him in the face. This is body language that indicates it's both of you together, against an unfriendly world.

• Don't look straight into the person's eyes. This may seem threatening. Look at some other point.

• Don't use words such as "I" and "you." Instead, try to use pronouns such as "he," "she" and "they."

- Try to share emotions. If the person is frustrated, you act frustrated. (This may not have to be that much of an act.)
- Be "a little paranoid" yourself. Although you should not lie, find something credible (if only mildly so) in what the individual is saying. Weiden says you may be able to draw your relative away from paranoia if you do it in a stepwise fashion, and denying the paranoid delusions altogether is too many steps away.

If you use this last suggestion, your mission is to actually get the individual to challenge what you are saying and to tell you that *you* are paranoid! For example, if a person says that the reason for his last hospitalization was a conspiracy by the police, you can agree and state that you think the police were at fault for many other problems as well, and cite a few. Your goal is to make the mentally ill individual tell you to stop picking on the police. Although this method may sound quirky and controversial, psychiatrists who have tried it insist that it has worked well for them.

ANGER AND VIOLENCE

Although most mentally ill people are far more likely to be victimized than to be violent, sometimes they can behave in a violent manner. In dealing with a violent person, do the following:

- Don't argue or be confrontational.
- Try to remain calm. Speak in a quiet and even voice.
- Don't touch or stare at the person.
- Do what the person wants if the request is not unreasonable.
- Position yourself so you can leave.

When You Have to Call 911

If you need help, get help. You may even need to call the police. If you call 911, don't use psychobabble such as "My son is decompensating"; instead, tell the person, "My son is mentally ill" or "My son is emotionally disturbed." If you have time, you could also provide some explanation, such as "My son says he's going to hurt me and he has done it before. I'm afraid."

When the Police Get There

As soon as the police arrive, tell them that your relative is a threat to himself and/or to you. This is what they need to hear in order to feel that they are not violating anyone's civil rights. It's also a good idea to hand them a Crisis Information Form, a form that you have prepared ahead of time and put in a safe place. This form provides the information they need to place your relative in a facility where he (and you) will be safe. It includes such information as the person's name, address, psychiatrist's name, medications the ill person takes, and other important data. (See the sample in Appendix C, which is adapted from a form produced by AMI/FAMI in New York.)

DENIAL

If your relative thinks there's nothing wrong with her and it must be *you* that has a problem, don't fight about it, particularly when the person is suffering from acute psychosis. And don't drag the person to a session with a psychologist; you'll gain nothing. Instead, take whatever action is necessary to maintain the safety of the ill person, yourself, and the family.

You can also try to accept the person's belief as one point of view, and tell her that. Then you may wish to suggest that there are other points of view. In one case, a hospitalized person told a psychiatrist, "You think I'm crazy, don't you?" Rather than answering directly, the doctor said, "Well, your chart indicates that you do have some symptoms."

Do recognize that denial of the illness may serve as a sort of shield for the individual. It is very painful for a person to admit that she is psychotic and may not be able to do the things that peers or siblings will be able to do, such as graduate from college, hold a good job, marry, have children, and so forth.

BLAMING EVERYTHING ON THE ILLNESS

Sometimes the person with the neurobiological disorder will believe that every problem and every deficit he has is a direct result of his illness. Do not allow this idea to stand; it can prevent your relative from trying and from achieving his potential. Talk about problems that you have had in your life, so your relative realizes that all is not rosy and perfect in the lives of those who are not mentally ill. Maybe you are a perfectionist or maybe you have trouble paying attention. Everyone has flaws. Without berating yourself, frankly discuss one of your flaws and how you think it may have held you back. The example you give should be significant—getting an "F" in geometry doesn't come close to experiencing a neurobiological disorder. Also, do not talk about subjects such as sexual behavior—your own or others'.

Praise the person's behavior when you can, and be sincere about your praise. Do not speak in a patronizing tone, the one you might use to talk to a small child.

REFUSAL TO SEE THE DOCTOR

Sometimes your relative may refuse to see the psychiatrist or therapist. Is the refusal reasonable? Perhaps the person doesn't like the doctor because the doctor is an authoritarian-type person and your relative would do better with a doctor who is more egalitarian in manner. Or perhaps your relative is just being argumentative and difficult, as everyone is once in a while. If she will still go with you, albeit grumbling, then take her. You might tell the person you are leaving, put on your coat and wait in the car. If she shows up, then go off together. If not, don't panic. Doctors and therapists know that sometimes mentally ill people are irrational, and you can call and explain.

If your relative is a child or adolescent, you can make her go to the doctor or therapist, albeit reluctantly. In fact, says Bert Warren, a psychiatrist in private practice in Fanwood, New Jersey, clinical director of the Union County Psychiatric Clinic in Plainfield, New

Jersey, and former president of the New Jersey Psychiatric Association, "In terms of children and adolescents, there are two types. There are volunteers and prisoners. Very often I will see these folks when they are in their teens and younger as prisoners."

Warren cites the case of an adolescent boy whose mother forced him to obtain treatment for his obsessive-compulsive disorder. "He didn't want to come see me at first and his mother had to drag him in." Then the boy got his license and he wanted the car, so going to the doctor was a good excuse to gain access to the car. "Now he's in college," says Warren. "At first he tried to do without the medicine and he found he needs it. So I started him on medication again. He was a prisoner and now he's a volunteer."

DISAGREEMENTS BETWEEN CAREGIVERS AND DOCTORS OR THERAPISTS

There may be times when the doctor tells you to do something—for example, he may want to change your relative's medication—and you will disagree. Or vice versa. Is the doctor, therapist, or social worker automatically right because of their special training? No. Sometimes they're wrong and sometimes they're right. What you need to do is carefully evaluate the doctor's request and your objections. Talk it over with the mental health professional. If you still disagree, ask your spouse or a trusted friend for an honest opinion.

Ask yourself these questions:

1. Could compliance be dangerous or harmful?
2. Does your relative agree with the mental health professional?
3. Would compliance be financially difficult? If so, what does the patient—and you—gain?
4. Will you be able to obtain help if there is a bad outcome to this treatment?

If you've answered "yes" to number one, then you must insist that the doctor or therapist tell you what to do if a serious problem occurs.

If you answered "yes" to the other questions, you need more information and help from the mental health professional on how to make compliance work.

GETTING THE INFORMATION YOU NEED

Although there may be state laws regarding confidentiality and the provision of information to family members, in most cases, the information could be provided. But what if the mental health professional, for various reasons, doesn't wish to provide it? This can be an extremely difficult situation. For example, you need to know what the medication is supposed to do and what the side effects are. If you are not told and the ill person complains repeatedly, then you as a caregiver may decide to take the person off the medication since it's not doing any good. This may—or may not—cause a relapse. You need accurate information to provide the best care. Don't settle for anything less.

In the case of a cancer patient, says Dr. Richard Keefe, Ph.D., author and assistant professor of psychiatry at the Mount Sinai School of Medicine in New York, "Doctors don't say, 'This is going to be between me and the cancer patient and you're not involved.'" Instead, he says that family members and caregivers are invited in by a compassionate physician who explains the problem to everyone. Of course, there are some issues of confidentiality that a therapist should respect, says Keefe. For example, if the patient wishes to talk about something very private, such as sexuality, that discussion should be between the therapist and the ill person. The psychiatrist, psychologist, or other therapist must exercise a certain amount of judgment.

KEEPING STRESS LEVELS DOWN

Many psychiatrists will caution family members to try to keep things as low-key as possible and to avoid "stress." But, says Dr. Weiden, "life is not a stress-free event. . . . If your schizophrenic relative sits in his room and watches the Phil Donahue show for the rest of his life, he might not ever get sick—but he won't have much of a life. Whereas, if he goes out and does things, he may have relapses. That's the tradeoff."

Weiden advises, instead, that you carefully consider, whenever you can, what events are worth the stress. For example, if your relative will be very stressed-out by having all the family over for the Christmas holidays, will it be worth it to you? "Maybe not," says Weiden. "But it might be worth stressing your relative to go out on a date so he can have a social life."

DEALING WITH MANIPULATIVE BEHAVIOR

Are you "giving in" to your relative too much and being manipulated—or is illness the problem? Often, it's hard to know. It's best to err on the conservative side and assume that your relative is not behaving manipulatively. But there are some signs you can look for. If your relative exhibits any or all of them, you are being manipulated and you must deal with it accordingly.

- The ill person says he can't eat dinner with the family because he's too upset, but a friend asks him to eat out and he wants to go.
- The ill person refuses to work, but demands money from the caregiver.
- The ill person refuses to do any chores around the home because he's too "sick," but if an interesting activity comes up, he is suddenly well.
- The ill person says she can't mow the lawn because it's too hard, but she will go bowling or play basketball.

Many "normal" people are manipulative, too. The mentally ill person who is manipulative uses her disease to avoid tasks that are unpleasant to her. Use money or candy as an inducement. As a last resort, you can also use housing: The person must comply with your rules if she wishes to continue living with you.

DEALING WITH PUBLIC OUTBURSTS

What do you do if your relative starts "freaking out" in the supermarket? Do you rush out? Do you hand him the car keys and tell him to go sit in the car? Do you tell people, "Excuse me, my son is having a drug reaction"? Depending on the situation, you may try some or all of these tactics.

Although your relative is your first concern and you should not worry excessively about what strangers think, sometimes you need to address them because they may react negatively to you or to your relative. Some people actually hand out cards, saying something like, "My son has a brain disorder and is under treatment." In some cases, mentally ill adults hand out their own cards. For example, if a person has Tourette's syndrome, he may unintentionally blurt out obscenities and insults—not always a safe thing to do, even if it is uncontrollable. He may find that passing out simple printed cards will avert a confrontation.

What you have to do is weigh maintaining the dignity of your relative with her imminent safety and well-being. So you probably would not pass out such cards in a place where your relative would be embarrassed—for example, in the school setting. (If the ill person chooses to pass out cards, that is her choice and that's fine.) Of course, you can also choose to ignore the behavior and walk away from the person. Or you may be successful with distracting him by looking at something that you suddenly find very interesting. A brief moment's distraction can be very effective.

9

PROBLEMS OF SPECIFIC TYPES OF CAREGIVERS

Parents, Spouses, Siblings, and Adult Children

How you cope with your relative will vary depending on whether the person is your child, spouse, sibling, or parent. Sometimes adjusting to your role as caregiver can be difficult, especially when you now have to care for the person who once cared for you, or when you must assume responsibility for the household if it is your spouse who is now ill. No matter what your situation, there will be difficult adjustments to make, both emotionally and physically.

CARING FOR YOUR SPOUSE

Although only an estimated 10 percent of severely mentally ill people are married, many of you will be spouses of mentally ill people. Perhaps the mental illness did not exist or was undetectable during "courting." Or it didn't seem severe if its existence was known.

"I probably wouldn't have even dated him if I knew he was a manic depressive," says M., who has been married to her husband for ten years. "I didn't know anything about mental illness and it would have scared me right off."

Her husband had been discharged from the Navy because he was "phobic" and the doctors said once he was out of the Navy, he'd be fine. "I thought it was more serious than that," she said. "But they wouldn't listen to me."

After surviving several years of both his manic behavior and his subsequent plummets into depression, M. put her foot down and told her husband he was going to have to see a psychiatrist or the marriage was over. He did, and medication helped him to regain his life—and save his marriage.

Telling Family Members

You may have an aversion to telling other family members about the illness, because you feel embarrassed or even disloyal. But they need to know, too. For example, some illnesses appear to be genetically based and thus can run in families. Family members deserve to know this information. (See Chapter 10 for more information.)

Dealing with Financial Loss

In about 40 percent of the cases, the family's financial situation deteriorates because the "breadwinner" becomes too ill to work—in some cases, the family income drops to half of what it has been. You will need to scale back and you may need to ask other family members for help. You should be sure to investigate such options as SSI and other programs, described in Chapter 17.

Social Isolation and Bereavement

Social isolation is a serious problem and a majority of caregivers experience a decrease in their social activities after their spouse becomes ill. Your spouse, whom you once treated as an equal, is now dependent on you. In addition, it may be hard for your spouse to face this fact. It's important to acknowledge that this is a difficult situation for you both.

Often, a couple's sexual relationship suffers as well. In many cases, couples stop having sex altogether and others report problems in this area of their marital life. Of course, it should be noted that the person with manic depression might demand *more* sex during manic phases.

General coping strategies that seem to work for ill spouses include thinking first before saying something, giving in to the spouse more frequently, and arguing less.

It's often difficult for the well spouse to gain support from the mentally ill spouse's family, who may think and even say, "He was fine before he married you!" And maybe he was fine, because the neurobiological disorder had not become evident yet. Or because it had been a mild problem to which they had all turned a blind eye but that can no longer be ignored. Don't accept blame from relatives, yours or your spouse's. Explain that the illness is a neurobiological disorder and is no one's "fault." Offer articles or books that they can read. If this doesn't work, you may need to distance yourself from them.

These are all difficult problems for a caregiving spouse, in addition to the stress, exhaustion, and frustration that all caregivers suffer. Education can help, as can educating others. Respites are important, as are finding outlets for your own creativity and enjoyment, an activity that is separate from the ill spouse.

CARING FOR A SIBLING

Sometimes adult siblings become caregivers when former caregivers become too old or too ill, or die. In many cases, the friendships or other relationships that mentally ill people may have are too tenuous (or nonexistent) to provide them with the caregiving and support they need. Many siblings, both male and female, do provide caregiving. But there are problems for the sibling caregiver. For example, siblings mourn for the person they once knew and they may resent their caregiving responsibilities. They may also experience "survivor guilt"—why him and not me? In addition, other siblings in the family may distance themselves from the ill person, which can be puzzling or upsetting to the sibling caregiver.

If your sibling was mentally ill when you were growing up, you may harbor some resentment for all the attention that person received from your parents. You may wonder if he was faking it or if she is really, truly ill. You may have delayed childbearing because you're afraid you might have defective genes that will be passed on to your offspring. Or maybe you still wonder if someday you might "break down."

One sibling was convinced that she could handle her sister when the group home didn't work out. Her mother begged her not to do it, not to take on this responsibility, but she wouldn't listen. Now that I'm an adult, doesn't my mother realize that I *can* handle this? she thought resentfully. What she found was that her mother knew that the sibling required far more care than a woman with a career and a family could handle on her own. After a short period, she gave up. She also finally realized what her mother had been through, all those years. The sister moved into a different group home.

If you are responsible for caring for a sibling, it's important to do the following:

- Understand that you will need to give up the former roles you had as children. Don't continue to be "big sister" or "little brother." Create a new relationship with the ill person. You are the caregiver, but that does not mean that, for example, big sister should run her sibling's life, particularly an adult's life.

- Acknowledge past resentments, and don't say there aren't any. They exist in every family. For example, if you thought the ill person got too much attention, accept those thoughts and let them go. If you thought he was Mom's favorite, maybe he was! Accept it and let it go. This is not easy. But I believe that it's important to create a good caregiving relationship. You will probably never be able to give up all the negative feelings, but by acknowledging them, you may be able to free yourself of many of them.

- Think about the good times you had with your sibling before the illness, times you had together as children and as adults (if your relative was well during adulthood). Allow yourself to grieve for the activities that you can no longer do together, and think about things that you can do together now. If you loved picnicking together as children, you could arrange to go on a picnic—in a secluded place if your sibling is paranoid or afraid of people. You may even be able to plan it together—where to go, what food to eat, when to do it, and so on.

- Whenever possible, find other family members who can give you back up help. Do *not* let your other siblings presume that you will do it all. And they will make this presumption unless you tell them otherwise. You don't have to be the "good" girl or boy all the time. Try not to pull rank as the main caregiver and order this sibling or that sibling to do the job. Instead, try a collaborative and negotiating approach. It works better!

- Give yourself credit for doing something really important, and appreciate yourself! Where would this person be if you were not providing care? In the streets? In a homeless shelter? Dead? Keep this in mind when the doubts crowd in about whether you are really doing a good job.
- Plan for the future. Make a plan for your relative for when you become incapacitated or die. Most caregivers report that they are terrified about what will happen to Jimmy or Jenny when the caregiver dies—yet they do nothing to prevent a shattering change for the relative when they are ultimately unable to provide care. Read Chapter 14 and create your own plan.

CARING FOR A CHILD

So many hopes and dreams are tied up in our children. We consider them beautiful and we assume they'll be wonderfully successful. We want them to be healthy and happy. If our children become mentally ill, no matter what the doctors tell us, almost invariably we become racked with guilt, fear, and self-doubt. What did we do to cause this? What can we do to fix it? And when acceptance slowly comes, we start to face other issues. Who will take care of the child when we die? Who will love the child? These are painful questions to face.

Here are some tactics for dealing with the day-to-day caregiving of a mentally ill child.

- Locate a good child psychiatrist. Do *not* rely on a psychiatrist who doesn't specialize in helping children. If you have to travel to consult with a child psychiatrist, do so. Use the guidelines offered in Chapter 4 for finding a psychiatrist. In addition, you could call The American Academy of Child and Adolescent Psychiatry at 202-966-7300 to obtain names of child psychiatrists in your area.
- Realize that it can be difficult to diagnose a child with a neurobiological disorder, even for a highly competent psychiatrist. Children may exhibit symptoms of a variety of illnesses; for

example, children with attention deficit disorder may also have a learning disability or a conduct disorder, as well as major depression and other problems. Don't expect immediate answers or quick fixes; however, do expect that your child will, at some point, achieve a higher level of wellness.

- Understand that the mental illness may affect the child's age-level behavior. For example, a child with a neurobiological disorder may act much younger than she actually is. Give simple instructions, tailored to the child's emotional age level. A child who has schizophrenia needs fewer and clearer instructions than a child of the same age without schizophrenia.

- Carefully consider psychiatric hospitalization before having your child admitted. There are some facilities that will admit children and adolescents who are "going through a difficult time" and having normal, albeit difficult, adjustments to life problems. They do this to fill up beds. (Often, such facilities launch advertising campaigns during summer vacations, promising you a "free evaluation.") It's better to pay a psychiatrist to evaluate your child and to obtain an objective analysis.

  If your child is not a danger to himself or others, hospitalization is probably not necessary. Get a second opinion. Unnecessary hospitalization can be very traumatic for your child and your family. On the other hand, if your child's life *is* in danger, hospitalization may be the only answer.

- Provide positive reinforcement whenever possible, but don't ignore discipline. Keep rules simple and punishments consistent.

- Protect yourself and your belongings. For example, if a child steals your money, jewelry, and other items of value, lock them up. Some people might say this indicates you don't trust the child. That is true; however, when your child was a toddler, did you lock up poisons so your child wouldn't consume them? The mentally ill person may have a similar overwhelming desire to take your personal belongings. Until and unless you can help the person overcome this behavior, take actions to care for your important items.

- Empathize with your child, but don't throw out all the rules because you feel sorry for him. Be kind and compassionate, but don't be a doormat. Your child continues to need a loving but firm parent.

- Make sure you get time off. Mentally ill children can be very demanding and exhausting, and you will need breaks.
- If the child throws a temper tantrum in a public place, leave when you can. Or, if the child is old enough, tell her to go wait outside or in the car. Don't worry about what everyone else thinks—they have probably seen temper tantrums before. If you are worried that someone will think you have abused the child, thus causing her reaction, you could say that the child is sick, has a neurobiological disorder, a migraine, or some other illness.
- Other children will probably tease your child. Empathize with her. Explain that all children get teased for some reason (wearing braces or glasses, being thin or fat) and what the children zero in on in her case is her mental illness. Talk about incidents when you were teased as a child. Know that her experience will probably be much harder to deal with than yours, because her thinking and reactions are impaired by the neurobiological disorder.
- Work with the school system. If your child remains in "regular" classes, talk with teachers and explain the problem. Know that some people will (at least initially) blame you for the problem. Talk to teachers and staff about the fact that you realize in the past people have blamed parents for all mental illnesses, but now it is known that mental illnesses are caused by problems in the brain that are independent of parents' actions or inactions. Present this view as the enlightened and educated view (which it is) and most educators will respond. If your child is in a special education class, don't assume that his teachers know everything about his particular disability. Provide them with information and education in a respectful manner.

CARING FOR A PARENT

Many adults are caught between their aging parents and their own children, born when they were in their late twenties or thirties. What should you do when your Mom or Dad can no longer function in their own home? Should you have them move in with you? The problem is complicated when the aging parent has a mental disorder. If it's a degenerative disorder such as Alzheimer's, the parent will become increasingly dependent. After a time, the parent will no longer recognize the child.

Here are some suggestions for dealing with an elderly relative who is mentally ill:

- Try to avoid criticism, such as yelling or threatening the person. Such behavior is common, but it only results in a greater emotional burden for the caregiver and a greater desire to institutionalize the relative.
- Use praise or positive words whenever possible and focus on the "bright side."
- If the physician agrees, create a simple exercise program for your relative. Dr. David Sudderth, a neurologist in Naples, Florida, says exercise will improve mental functioning and may also help the person sleep better at night.
- Provide simple mental "calisthenics," such as crossword puzzles or other noncomplex challenges, says Dr. Sudderth. These enjoyable tasks can effectively exercise the brain.
- Avoid upsetting situations. Some people become upset if they are approached suddenly, if they are rushed, if people speak to them rudely, or if a situation is too confusing. Sometimes television programs upset elderly people with mental problems, especially those who have trouble determining whether television programs are real. Talk to the person calmly, especially when he is upset. If that doesn't work, try distracting the person and return to the desired activity later.
- Avoid arguments. Try to accept what the ill person is saying, even if you know it is wrong, rather than arguing. (This may also work with a paranoid person. Arguing never works.)
- Physical contact is also often effective. Hug the ill person, hold her hand or give her a pet to hold. (Note: This tactic will not work with a paranoid person who wants "hands off.")
- If you can, go along with a situation. One woman whose mother constantly asked to "go home" found that it didn't work when she tried to convince her mother that she *was* home. So she took her mother for a short ride in the car, pointed out landmarks, and then stated that soon they would be home. Then they'd drive back to the house and the mother would be all right.
- Allow the mentally ill person to do what she wants to do as long as it is not harmful. For example, one woman was convinced that

someone was coming for lunch every day, and would spend a great deal of time setting the table, no matter how hard her husband tried to convince her that no one was coming. He finally decided to help her with this task, and then before noon, he would tell his wife that their "lunch guests" had canceled and she should put the items away.

- Distract the person. For example, in one case, a mentally ill person was demanding that the mail carrier release her son from the back of his truck. (She was hallucinating.) Several neighbors calmly engaged the woman in a discussion about her son, and waved the mailman away until the woman's son came to help her.
- Play soothing music. Music works very well in calming agitated people. This should be music that the ill person likes—this is *not* the time to "broaden his or her taste in music."

10

DEALING WITH PEOPLE OUTSIDE THE IMMEDIATE FAMILY

Here's what *not* to do when you are a caregiver to a mentally ill person: Hide this fact. Don't tell anybody. If someone asks you a question, change the subject. Tell your children that they may not tell anyone what has happened. This is an ineffective tactic—and a common one. I did it, but no longer. Instead, tell people that your family member has a neurobiological disorder, and if they ask what that is, explain.

Why do we fear telling others? Because of the social stigma and because we allow ourselves to be ashamed and embarrassed. Of course, you don't need to tell people you're standing next to in an elevator or strangers or people you barely know that you have a mentally ill relative. If it comes up and you want to talk about it, fine. If not, that is okay, too. But there are people whom you associate with on a regular basis who wonder what is going on, and they will appreciate any information that you provide. By sharing your knowledge and experiences, you have the chance to educate people about neurobiological disorders.

HOW THE ILLNESS AFFECTS OTHER RELATIVES

When you finally tell other family members about your relative's neurobiological disorder, you can expect shock, dismay, sympathy, blame—the whole range of reactions. You may also find that your extended family is far more supportive than you imagined. You may find, to your surprise, that there are other family members with serious problems who were afraid to tell anyone else in the family. Now the secret can at last be shared.

There may also be a feeling of disbelief among your relatives. How could this happen in *our* family? Doesn't this only happen to other people? And, oh God, what if this bad thing happens to my kids or even to me? As a result, it's a good idea to share the information you learn with other family members.

It's disappointing, but true, that some of your distant relatives and friends may stop seeing you socially. They may even pretend not to see you on the street or actively avoid you. This hurts. One woman told me of her very close relationship with her large extended family and many friends, and who enjoyed regular socializing. Her son was popular with extended family members and her friends, and they clearly enjoyed his presence at birthday parties, holidays, and other events. Then her son became psychotic. In one incident, he was arrested for not paying for a meal in a restaurant. This woman's friends and extended family heard about what was happening. "When he got sick, they didn't know him and didn't want to know us anymore. They just dropped us," the mother said, her pain evident in her voice.

You can hope that with time, friends and relatives will see the error of their ways and come back. But you can't count on it and you can't force it to happen.

Other Relatives' Concerns

Relatives may worry about the ill person, and how the caregivers are handling the situation. Grandparents often worry about their adult children and how they are holding up in caring for the mentally ill grandchild. Relatives may criticize the caregiver directly, offering well-meaning advice that will not help. Love the ill person more. Coddle him less. Send him off to work. Help her find some new friends or interests. If any of these were possible and the ill person would cooperate, most caregivers have already tried the suggested tactics.

Just as the immediate caregivers wonder if and how they may have caused the problem, so do extended family members. Even if everyone accepts the biological model and believes that neurobiological diseases are not anyone's fault, relatives may begin to dissect the family tree to see who was mentally ill, who was a little strange, and who is normal. They may also worry about whether their own children might be vulnerable to the illness, or whether they themselves are ticking time bombs, waiting to explode into psychosis. These are all terrifying (and common) fears.

ASK RELATIVES AND CLOSE FRIENDS FOR HELP

While you will receive negative reactions from some relatives and friends, others will be very supportive. In fact, you may be able to convince a relative or friend to take care of your ill relative for at least a few days. As some of my interviewees found, relatives who didn't believe the person was really sick—or who provided lots of unhelpful advice—were humbled by the experience of caring for the ill person. They had a far greater appreciation of the caregiver after "walking in her shoes," and in some cases, they bought into the problem and continued to help.

You may also find, to your surprise, that relatives and friends have had similar experiences, but they were afraid to tell anyone about it. After you share information, they are far more likely to open up about their own caregiving experiences and share with you what has worked well for them.

11

BALANCING WORK AND CAREGIVING

M any caregivers find that they must give up their jobs or work at home, while others struggle to continue their full-time or part-time employment. Of those who continue to work, about 80 percent report a deterioration in their work performance. Herein lies the dilemma. If you have to give up or cut back on work, this can lead to financial problems, further increasing your overall stress level.

It's hard enough to cope with the needs of a mentally ill person. The stresses and struggles of most careers add a further burden. On the other hand, if you stop working, who is going to pay the bills?

STRATEGIES FOR COMBINING WORK AND CAREGIVING

If you find that your caregiving duties are affecting your work, try these suggestions:

- Tell your boss that you care for a mentally ill relative. Many people try to conceal this information from their supervisor, believing that it would be detrimental in some way. But if your boss doesn't know the reason for sudden absences, personal calls, and so forth, what is the boss to think? Rather than allow speculation, briefly provide a simple explanation.
- Set aside time to work and time to worry. Sometimes it helps to compartmentalize your problems—this is what works for me. If

you constantly think about how terrible your problem is or rack your brains about what you are going to do with the ill person, you are not going to be a very effective worker. Instead, concentrate on work when you are at work. When thoughts of the ill person come up, tell yourself you will think about that later— when you get home or tonight or some other time. It sounds like procrastination or like Scarlett O'Hara in *Gone With the Wind*. But I don't think it is—it is a coping mechanism.

- Plan ahead. Making a plan for handling the problems that worry you will also help you perform better in the workplace. For example, if you are worried about what would happen to your relative if you were to become sick or to die, then make a plan for what would happen in that event. Read Chapter 14 in this book and talk to support group members. Find a good estate planning attorney. Once you have made a plan, you will have one less worry.

- Consider taking time off under the Family and Medical Leave Act. If your relative should become ill and need your services, the Family and Medical Leave Act provides for up to 12 weeks of unpaid leave for most employees. (Some small businesses are exempt. Check with your employer for details.) Note that these are *unpaid* weeks, so you may prefer to use up your vacation time first.

  Be sure to give your employer information on what the problem is and make it clear that you need to provide care to your relative. Your relative's age doesn't matter. You are entitled to this unpaid leave under the Family and Medical Leave Act if this person is dependent on you for care. Although your employer can hire a temporary worker to fill in for you while you are gone, your employer must take you back in the same position you held before when the leave is up.

12

WHEN THE MENTALLY ILL PERSON HOLDS A JOB

A lthough many, perhaps the majority, of people with mental illness cannot work, it's important to try to help those who can find a work niche. Many want to earn a paycheck and feel important. In addition, the structure of a regular work schedule can improve self-esteem and reinforce a regular meal and medication schedule.

MYTHS ABOUT MENTALLY ILL PEOPLE AND WORK

Rehabilitation experts say that one problem confronting mentally ill people and their caregivers is the mythology surrounding mentally ill people and work. Although you can't expect a mentally ill person to go out and get a full-time job with no repercussions, experts insist that "supported employment," with available counselors and experts—for example, the Fountain House program, described in this chapter—can provide a suitable work environment.

One myth is that mentally ill people will become worse and worse (the "abandon all hope" philosophy). This belief is very detrimental to assisting a mentally ill person in a supported employment job. A longitudinal study at Vermont State Hospital revealed that over 50 percent of the people with schizophrenia improved or recovered over the course of 20 years, disproving the downward trend belief.

Another myth is that mentally ill people are too delicate to cope with a supported employment job. However, mentally ill people *can* be taught coping skills. Do not judge how the person will do by the first few days of work. Most people find starting a new job stressful and this is a normal reaction, not a psychotic one at all.

Of course there is also the myth that mentally ill people are invariably aggressive, hostile, and dangerous—not desirable attributes in an employee. And not true, either. This myth is prevalent in our society and groups such as the National Alliance for the Mentally Ill (NAMI) actively fight against it.

THE AMERICANS WITH DISABILITIES ACT

People with neurobiological disorders are disabled, and are therefore protected under the Americans with Disabilities Act (ADA) from discrimination in employment. This Act was passed in 1990; in 1994, it was extended to all employers with 15 or more workers.

The problem is that if the mentally ill person wants the work environment changed or adapted to his needs, then the fact of the mental illness must be presented to the employer. In several lawsuits that were lost, the person did not tell the employer about the illness. For example, in 1994, a Maryland woman who was terminated from her job said she suffered discrimination because of her manic depression. Her employer said he did not know she was disabled and she was fired because she was loud and abusive. The court upheld the termination based on the woman's misconduct and her withholding of information about her disability.

Telling others that they have a mental illness is hard for many people because they don't want to be stigmatized. Nor do they want co-workers to presume that they are or will be incompetent at best and a knife-wielding assailant at worst. Each person must come to some decision about the tradeoffs involved in such disclosure. In one case, a postal worker was fired, apparently because he had told his supervisor he suffered from posttraumatic stress syndrome. After several postal workers became violent and homicidal, his supervisor feared that this person, who had lost his temper several times, might also lose control and murder people. The court upheld the worker's claim because he continued to perform well and it was unfair to generalize from other people's behavior and to stigmatize this worker.

If the person needs a calm, structured environment with periodic breaks, and this is not the norm in the workplace (although it could be readily accommodated), that person must tell the employer what is needed. Disclosure, however, may be difficult. Mentally ill people do not have to tell the employer everything about the illness; they need only to provide information about those aspects that create a need for accommodation. They can also ask that others in the company not be told and that their privacy be respected.

For further information, contact the ADA Regional Disability and Technical Assistance Center at 800-949-4232 or the Job Accommodation Network at 800-ADA-WORK.

FINDING AND KEEPING A JOB

Finding work and staying in a job can be very difficult for a person with a mental illness. Why? Employers expect people to arrive at work on time and do their jobs with minimal supervision. They don't like long and unanticipated absences. In addition, employers dislike strange behavior.

What Kind of Job?

Because people with mental illnesses have wide variations of intelligence, although most are of normal intelligence, you might think that some could handle somewhat difficult jobs. But job stress is an important factor. The best type of job for a person with schizophrenia is one that is somewhat repetitive and low stress, with little time pressure. Yet such a job may be boring for a bright person and is usually low paying, problems that are hard to solve.

VOCATIONAL REHABILITATION

Most states have several vocational rehabilitation programs. Usually they have one program for the blind and another program for all others with disabilities. Your adult relative may be eligible if a disability prevents him from getting a job, and he could get a job after participating in a "voc rehab" program. Check the phone book for the nearest vocational rehabilitation office. This office can tell you what paperwork and information they need in order to determine your relative's eligibility for their program.

Programs may include on-the-job training, or your relative may be sent to a local institution to obtain the necessary training. Work experience training may be provided for the person who has never worked and needs help with basic work, social, and interpersonal skills. If your relative is accepted into the program, she will receive an Individualized Written Rehabilitation Program (IWRP).

Clubhouses

There are an estimated 600+ facilities that offer a transition to the workplace. One key program is Fountain House, based in New York City. This organization has programs internationally and in 40 states, serving 20,000 people altogether. There are other clubhouses, too, and experts say that in most cases you can find a clubhouse program in your general area. Some members live at the facility while others do not.

Clubhouses range from those that offer a concentration on jobs to those with more of a day treatment/therapy orientation. You may not be able to get your relative into your first choice program because there is plenty of competition for these slots. Contact the Department of Mental Health in your state to locate the clubhouses in your area. Note: Many outpatient programs call themselves clubhouses but do not meet Fountain House standards. Call Fountain House at 212-582-0340 to see whether a clubhouse meets their standards.

Clubhouses for seriously mentally ill people can provide a transition between the world of volunteer work supervised or managed by clubhouse leaders and independent, paid employment. Nearly all of the people who come to Fountain House as members are severely mentally ill with such neurobiological diseases as schizophrenia or manic depression. Fountain House in New York City, which is open 365 days a year, has placed their members in entry-level jobs at such companies as the Wall Street Journal, Fox Television, and four big law firms. They also offer a full-time placement service. A good program, say experts, is defined as having a work program in the community—real jobs in real businesses.

Membership is free and members are members for life (although eventually some members drop out or no longer participate). Members are encouraged to do volunteer work; since they are receiving free services, they can pay in terms of "sweat equity."

Fountain House has about 200 facilities around the globe; however, there are many clubhouses who use the Fountain House name or say that they follow the Fountain House international standards. (All Fountain House clubhouses approved as of this writing are listed in Appendix J.) About half the Fountain House clubhouses in the United States are funded through Medicaid, and it is not certain what the future status of this program will be, although some facilities may close if funding is cut.

Clubhouse members must be at least 18 years old; there is no upper age limit, but most are in their 20s, 30s, and 40s. Members come from local state hospitals, shelters, and families. Unfortunately, Fountain House can't accommodate all the people who would like to participate in their program. The New York Fountain House receives about 100 referrals each month but can only accept about 20. (Call them each month to see if there's an opening.)

All the work of operating the clubhouse is done by staff and members. There are ten work units throughout the house and most people start with voluntary work at Fountain House. Then when they express interest in a regular job, Fountain House gives them that opportunity. Fountain House also offers an education program to assist people in earning their G.E.D. if they haven't finished high school or to help them reenter college.

If a person at Fountain House relapses and must go to a psychiatric facility, she may come back to Fountain House upon recovery. In some cases, the person can continue on with Fountain House even while at the psychiatric hospital; for example, if a person is hospitalized at Manhattan Psychiatric Center, a van is provided to drive the person back and forth from Fountain House to the hospital.

If basic issues, such as cleanliness, are a problem, the Fountain House staff works on them. For example, when someone expresses interest in getting a paid job, if cleanliness is a problem, the staff will tell the person that she must deal with this before going out for a job. People who have only been to the clubhouse intermittently for a few weeks may be told that the clubhouse staff needs more time to get to know them before they are taken out on a job.

WORK AND SSI

Often caregivers worry that if the mentally ill person begins to work, she runs the risk of losing not only the small disability check she receives from the Social Security Administration but also the Medicaid that covers her health problems and the cost of medications.

The Social Security Administration developed the "Plans for Achieving Self-Support Plan" or "PASS Plan" about 20 years ago; unfortunately for many, it has been a well-kept secret. This nationwide plan makes it possible for individuals to set aside a portion of their earnings for a goal such as going to college or purchasing a home computer to do their homework. Thus, the person will not automatically be bounced off SSI for exceeding whatever the resource limit is this year. In addition, the ill person's check would not be reduced by the amount of other income earned, but would stay the same. The PASS Plan must be submitted in writing to the Social Security Administration. Ask your local Social Security office about the PASS Plan and where to submit the written plan.

Extensions are also available; thus, your relative may be able to set aside money for important and feasible goals for up to four years. A plan that sounds workable and reasonable to the average person would probably satisfy the Social Security Administration workers, too. For further information on applying for SSI, see Chapter 17. It's also interesting to note that as of this writing, the Social Security Administration is testing a variation of the PASS Plan, wherein Social Security workers assist recipients in designing a feasible plan. One of the test sites is Tampa, Florida.

13

WHEN YOUR RELATIVE IS TOO ILL TO CARE FOR AT HOME

No matter how hard you try and how effective you are as a caregiver, there are times when you just cannot cope with your mentally ill relative any longer. Perhaps you are sick and worn out. Maybe you just need a break for a few days or a few weeks. Or perhaps the person needs a much higher level of care than you can possibly provide; for example, you cannot be on a 24-hour suicide watch for very long.

Try to evaluate—and this can be hard—if what you need is a respite of a few days or a week or if you truly cannot provide caregiving anymore, even if you have some time off. In some cases, hospitalization may be the answer, but do keep in mind that most hospitals will not involuntarily admit patients unless they are a danger to themselves or others. In other cases, you might need to place your relative in a group home or some other facility.

NURSING HOMES

If the ill person is elderly and you are considering a nursing home, that too can be a difficult decision. You may become overwhelmed with guilt, panic, and a broad array of other emotions. You may not get much help from others. People who have not been caregivers to

149

a mentally ill relative may be quick to tell you that *they* would *never* put their relative in an institution.

It's not easy to decide that you can no longer cope. "There are many emotional factors at play," says David Sudderth, M.D., a neurologist in Naples, Florida who is experienced in dealing with the families of the elderly and infirm. He suggests that signing your spouse into a nursing home is the last loss before the grave. As a result, you may feel intense guilt. In addition, says Dr. Sudderth, some people see this as an act of betrayal. Maybe the couple made vows to each other—"I'll never put you in a nursing home"—but there's simply no way out now.

As you can see, the decision won't be easy. But, again, you must do what is best for your relative as well as for yourself. If you are faced with this decision, weigh the pros and cons and talk to a professional about your feelings of guilt. Cover all the bases so that you won't have to second-guess yourself over whether you made the wrong decision.

RESIDENTIAL TREATMENT CENTERS

There are residential treatment facilities throughout the United States for children and adults. These are long-term facilities where people receive psychiatric treatment and medication. In most cases, they have long waiting lists. They are also generally very costly and their services are not covered by private health insurance. In some cases, expenses are covered by Medicaid.

DAY TREATMENT

If your relative does not need hospitalization but is having some serious problems that you think might result in this if they are not addressed, day treatment in a psychiatric facility may be the answer. In a day treatment setting, the person is there all day, often for a few more hours than the average work day for most people.

Depending on the program, mentally ill people may receive individual and group counseling and participate in a variety of activities. The goal is to stabilize them so they do not get worse and need to be hospitalized. Your insurance company may be willing to pay for day treatment because it is much less costly than hospitalization. It is primarily psychiatric hospitals that offer day treatment programs, although there are some other facilities that offer these services as well.

Note: For information on involuntarily hospitalizing your relative (formerly called "committing"), see Chapter 15.

14

PLANNING FOR YOUR RELATIVE'S FUTURE

One of the caregiver's greatest concerns is who will take care of the person with the neurobiological disorder when she is no longer around—when she is too ill to provide care or has died. As sad as it is to plan now, it is far better to make a plan than to assume that you will be well and live on indefinitely and let whatever happens happen. This is not fair to the person you love, the person who has depended on you.

Yet many families are guilty of *not* planning for the future. They worry about it plenty, but they don't *do* anything. Do not make this mistake! I'm sure you don't want your relative to be homeless, wandering the streets and depending on the charity of strangers. As you care for your relative now, care for him in the future by consulting a good attorney experienced in estate planning and making a plan for the future.

WILLING MONEY TO YOUR RELATIVE

The obvious drawback to leaving large sums of money to your mentally ill relative is that most people who are psychotic have difficulty handling money. (In fact, many people who are *not* psychotic make mistakes when they inherit money.) It's also not a good idea to make your ill relative your beneficiary. In addition, if your relative is on SSI or other programs and you leave him large sums of money, he may become ineligible. Then he will have to reapply for the pro-

153

grams at a later date (when the money is gone). Your lawyer will cover all of these points with you.

LEAVING MONEY TO ANOTHER RELATIVE

Another option is willing your money to the ill person's sibling or to some other person whom you trust. This could still be a problem if, for example, you leave the money to Mary, the sister of your mentally ill son Bill, and she dies. Unless her will is carefully written (and sometimes even if it is), her children and spouse could inherit everything and Bill would be left out in the cold. Again, a lawyer will help you cover these contingencies.

In addition, sometimes when people inherit money, they forget the promises they made to the ones who left them the money and they may not do as they promised. This means that Mary could decide that Bill doesn't need the money as much as she does. Again, Bill gets nothing. (It's not nice to think that way, but such things happen.) Make sure any arrangement you make covers all the bases and is legally sound.

GUARDIANSHIP

You should also be thinking about who should become the ill person's guardian when you are no longer able to function in this role, if a legal guardianship is indicated. Preferably, this would be a person your relative knows and trusts. Don't assume that adult siblings or other relatives will accept this responsibility: Ask them first and assure them that you will still love them if they say no. If you get a tentative "yes," explain what being a guardian entails.

What rights and responsibilities the guardian incurs varies drastically from state to state, and different guardian options may be available in the same state. For example, the guardian may be appointed primarily or solely to handle the ill person's financial affairs. Although many mentally ill people are not affluent, some are and they could theoretically make disastrous financial decisions on their own. Thus, a guardian could avert such a problem. Or the guardian may be in more of a caregiving role, offering advice and ensuring that the ill person's medical needs are looked after.

In some states, according to Robert J. Kaplan, staff attorney for the National Alliance for the Mentally Ill, guardians are also legally authorized to make treatment decisions for the ill person, for example, to obtain treatment on an outpatient basis. If the person fails to receive the treatment, then the guardian may provide consent for the person to be committed to a psychiatric facility. Again, a lawyer will help you sort this out.

PLANNED LIFETIME ASSISTANCE NETWORK (PLAN)

Organizations to care for your ill relative after your death exist (and are growing) throughout the United States. These organizations promise to provide a social worker to see your relative at least monthly and to check on him or her and essentially act as you would have acted had you done monthly visits. These organizations were originally formed by caregivers to mentally ill people.

Basically, what you do is pay an up front-fee and leave a life insurance policy to the PLAN group, which they will draw on to care for your relative for the rest of his or her life, including the home visits, working with social service agencies, arranging for intervention in crisis situations, and other services. The caregiver provides comprehensive information to the PLAN group—often the caregiver has many years of knowledge about the person in her or his head and this can be offered up so that the ill person's care can be tailored to her needs. (See the list of PLAN groups in Appendix H.)

PART THREE

THE SYSTEM MAY OR MAY NOT BE THE SOLUTION

How to Cope with Red Tape and Bureaucracies

This section is dedicated to practical problems that real people have faced in dealing with various legal and social systems, including the psychiatric hospital system, the mental health professional system, the educational system (if your relative is still attending school), and the insurance system.

For example, if you are still paying your relative's medical bills, sometimes dealing with the hospital's or doctor's billing department can be difficult. Sometimes it's the little things that get you. But there are good strategies for coping with such everyday problems.

Don't expect to find all the answers to every problem that anyone could face. My goal here is to get you started and to educate you about available resources and tactics.

15

THE PSYCHIATRIC
HOSPITAL SYSTEM

Welcome to the modern psychiatric hospital, here to treat your mentally ill relative with group and individual therapy, medication, and perhaps art therapy (making objects out of clay or other tasks). Some are reputable and some are not. These facilities care for people with mental illnesses. There are psychiatric hospitals for children and for adults. Sometimes people with problems of substance abuse are also treated in these facilities.

These facilities may be public, such as state hospitals, or they may be privately owned and run. In the past, many severely mentally ill people remained in state hospitals for their entire lives, but this is far less likely today. With the increasing push toward "managed care," hospital stays are far shorter than in the past and may be for days or weeks rather than months. Today people are discharged "sicker and quicker." Some psychiatric facilities offer partial hospitalization and/ or day treatment programs. This is an option for a person who is still ill but does not need to remain in the hospital overnight. (Insurance companies much prefer these programs to inpatient programs because the cost is lower.) The person in a partial hospitalization program may receive basically the same services as an inpatient except for any programs that occur at night.

The day treatment program may be less intensive, or it may be equal to what is provided by a partial hospitalization program. It's very important to ask for specifics about the program, including what services will be provided, what fees the relative may be expected to pay, and so on. Assume nothing.

PROBLEMS YOU MAY EXPERIENCE WITH HOSPITALS

Although psychiatric hospitals are very different—for example the private psychiatric hospital is different from the state hospital, and both are different from the psychiatric wing of a community hospital—there are some common problems you may experience.

Limited Visiting Hours

Many families complain that if their relative was sick in the local hospital, they could visit every day for hours. But if your relative is in a psychiatric hospital, you may be able to visit only several times a week for an hour or so, and visits may be semisupervised by staff members. Some people believe this is part of the "blame the family" syndrome—they don't want you coming in and upsetting the sick person even more, and they may be right. Others think the limited visiting hours are for the convenience of staff members—they don't have to keep track of who is where if everyone is locked up in their wards instead of visiting their families. Another reason for limited visiting hours is that the staff may plan special meetings or activities during the evening.

Language Barriers

A common complaint of families with a hospitalized relative is that the doctor speaks very broken English. The family can't understand him (it is almost invariably a male doctor) and he can't understand them. Or perhaps your relative is the one who speaks another language and is unable to communicate with the physician. This situation can be dangerous because patients can't communicate serious problems they're having with side effects from medications, nor can they verbalize questions or concerns and receive answers. A non-English speaking doctor may be highly competent, but if communication is impossible, this severely hampers treatment.

If your relative is assigned a doctor you cannot understand, don't be compliant. Ask him to print out what he wants you to know and you should write him notes. Better yet, go up the chain of command at the hospital and ask, in writing, for someone who can communicate to you what the doctor is saying, or request that your relative be assigned a different doctor. (It's a scary thought, but the staff probably doesn't understand him either.)

If it is your relative who cannot speak English, seek help. If you cannot provide translations, find someone who can. Perhaps there are others in your family who would be willing to help.

Committing Your Relative to a Hospital Involuntarily

You may believe, in fact you may be certain, that your relative needs to be hospitalized, based on your observations and past experience. If she agrees, you should be successful. If she does not agree, you have a problem. The basic law in most states is that a person may not be committed to a psychiatric facility involuntarily unless that person is a threat to himself or other people. Some states will allow an involuntary hospitalization if the person's illness makes him "gravely disabled" if not dangerous, says DePaul University law professor Samuel Jan Brakel.

Brakel notes that it was easier to involuntarily hospitalize people about 25 or 30 years ago. The need for treatment based on the person's mental illness was generally all that was required, and that need was substantiated by a psychiatrist or a committee of psychiatrists. The state acted within its *parens patriae* (state as parent) powers. Today, the judicial route is the only way to involuntarily hospitalize people. Brakel says that a few states are moving back to the "best interest" form of commitment and they have "resurrected the need-for-treatment standard as at least one criterion to be considered in commitment decisions, hopefully moving away from the idea of mental health commitment as strictly a police or public safety act."

If the person is violent, he may be taken to a psychiatric facility on an emergency basis for two to three days and later committed for a longer period by the court. "The problem, I think, is that the general narrowing of the commitment criteria with their emphasis, if not exclusive focus, on dangerousness has made the law both less usable and less used," says Brakel. He believes that the police are reluctant to take a person to the hospital involuntarily, "because they believe, or know from experience, that the hospital only takes a few of the worst cases, or that it discharges people the next day." In addition, the police officer who takes the person to the hospital may have to sit and wait for hours before any action is taken.

According to Brakel, what motivates the physicians who do admit patients depends on the doctor's view of the law, the scarcity of resources, and other issues. The basic underlying legal philosophy about involuntary hospitalizations today is that in most states, the person must be a danger to himself or to others before hospitalization can be involuntarily forced. And the definition of "danger" varies greatly from state to state, or even from judge to judge within a state.

Even when you believe that your ill relative *is* a danger to you or to himself, others may not believe you, as many people have told me. For example, if your relative is violent, did anybody besides you see the violence? Has the person actually committed any violent acts or is he merely threatening to do so? Are you overreacting? Unless there was a witness or you have proof of violence, you will have a hard time convincing anyone. Even when dangerously aggressive behavior does occur, it is possible that by the time the police get there, the person will have temporarily calmed down. In other situations, the person may be so depressed that he is refusing all food; still, he may look all right to the average person, and may not appear to be an immediate "threat" to himself. Some distraught caregivers turn over some chairs before the police come and say that the ill person did it. They justify this lying by convincing themselves that this is the only way to get the mentally ill person help.

Other problems with involuntary treatment, especially when mentally ill people reside with their caregiving families, involve the confidentiality issue, the fact that information about adult patients can be withheld from families, and the fact that often medications cannot be forced. If families have no idea what is going on with their involuntarily committed relatives, they will be ill-prepared to deal with the relative at home upon release.

Untangling Red Tape

If you are unhappy with some aspect of the treatment your relative is receiving (medication, a particular doctor's treatment, release from the hospital or admission, and so forth) and you are convinced that a change is in order, there are actions you can take to force such a change. These actions are punitive and threatening in nature and many people are extremely hesitant or even fearful to try them, thinking that the ill person will be retaliated against. In reality, this is unlikely. Instead, if you complain, the "system" is much more willing to take you seriously and give your relative the quality care you demand.

- Try to convince the person with the power to change whatever you believe needs to be changed.
- If that doesn't work, write a calm and rational letter to the person's boss's boss—two levels up from the person who refuses to take the action you want. In addition, write a letter to the head of the hospital and send copies to everyone below him or her. Send all letters at the same time. Also, if you are a NAMI member, send a copy of your letter to both your local chapter and the state AMI office.
- Complain to the Patients Rights Coordinator at the hospital by phone. Explain your position and follow up with a copy of your letter.
- Notify all letter recipients that you will send a copy of your letter to the state Commissioner of Mental Health if you do not receive satisfaction within a certain time frame (24 to 48 hours, or more). Judge the urgency of the situation. If they don't give you what you want, do send that letter, with a cover letter, to the state Mental Health Department.
- If this is an insurance-related matter, be sure to state in your letter that you will complain to the Insurance Commissioner if you do not receive satisfaction within some time period (a few days). If they don't give you what you want, do write to the Insurance Commissioner.
- Call the state Advocacy Center for disabled people and see if they would be willing to help you. Every state has an office that can provide legal advice or assistance to disabled people. These offices are usually located in the state capitol. They are often called "Protection and Advocacy" or "P&A" offices. Note: They would probably be more helpful to you in getting a person out of the hospital than in getting her admitted.
- When you get what you want, send a letter to everyone you wrote to before, thanking them for their help in resolving the problem, even if they didn't help. This is an important step! People want to know what happened to a complaint. If you ever need to take

these actions again, and you did *not* tell everyone what happened to your previous complaint, they may not take you seriously.

Coping With the Billing Department

One problem I've encountered over several years of bill paying for psychiatric and psychological services is difficulties and errors with billing. Despite sophisticated computer systems, and sometimes *because* of them, you may find some serious financial errors. You may encounter similar billing problems with medical clinics.

The most common billing problems I have encountered are over-billing and the failure to post payments that were made to my daughter's account. In several instances, the insurance company erred—for example, they sent my daughter's payment to the wrong psychiatrist, someone we'd never seen, and refused to pay the doctor that she *was* seeing. In another case, the psychologist's office lost my checks and asked me to write new ones. Apparently, an employee had misplaced all the checks for several weeks and they were never recovered.

My advice is to save all your cancelled checks, receipts, and any notices that you receive from the insurance company. Keep them all for at least a year, if not longer. You may find that someone new comes in, does an "audit" and decides you owe money that you feel you do *not* owe. Be prepared to back up your claim. This means you should take the time to set up and maintain a workable home filing system, because the amount of paperwork generated by hospitals, doctors, and insurance companies can seem beyond belief.

If you feel that you have identified a billing error, be polite and speak to the person at the billing department about the problem. Often you can solve the problem with one quick phone call. But if you can't, ask to speak to a supervisor. If all else fails and you receive no cooperation, write a letter to the head of the billing department of the hospital or psychiatric service.

You can also contact your insurance company, explain the problem, and try to identify what it is they need that they are not getting from the doctor. (Doctors are known as "providers" to insurance companies.) Yes, the insurance company and the doctor's office are supposed to communicate with each other. But sometimes there's animosity between them and they just don't. You can make them do so by interceding, if necessary.

I believe that simple courtesy and understanding will usually evoke a positive response; however, some people, frankly, respond better to threats. For example, one woman who was giving me a particularly difficult time over an erroneous bill completely changed her tone of voice and her attitude when I told her that I was going to ask the doctor what to do about the problem. Invoking the doctor's name is a powerful strategy! Even if you think the doctor wouldn't care or wouldn't do anything, it still might work. (Incidentally, these tactics also work with medical billing problems that have nothing to do with mental illness.)

IF THE HOSPITAL REFUSES TO TAKE YOUR ILL RELATIVE

Sometimes a psychiatric hospital may deny treatment, even when the ill person requests it. It could be a matter of economics—somebody has to pay the costs, whether it's you, the state, or some other agency. If you are concerned that your relative is suicidal and a facility still won't admit her, demand to see the hospital administrator. Tell the hospital administrator that the ill person is being placed at great risk of suicide and/or physical violence. Be sure to add that failure to admit this person will expose the hospital to a future lawsuit. It's important to be direct and confrontational.

16

THE EDUCATIONAL SYSTEM

Mentally ill children or adolescents can sometimes continue to attend classes with the other students. Sometimes they can't. This chapter covers educational needs and issues for children and adolescents, as well as for adults—college educations are also interrupted by a psychotic break and subsequent mental illness.

For about six months, my daughter was unable to attend school, because she simply could not cope with other people, especially adolescents her own age. So a teacher came to our house several times a week and provided private lessons until Jane could return to school. She kept up with the other students and returned at grade level.

In the past, kids such as Jane, and others like her, lost their opportunity for an education. But in 1975, the Education for All Handicapped Children Act, Public Law 94–142, was passed. The name of this law was later changed to The Individuals with Disabilities Education Act (IDEA). This law guarantees disabled students the right to an education in the "least restrictive environment." What is meant by "least restrictive environment" has been widely disputed. In some areas, it's presumed that the child should be placed in "regular" classrooms and everyone else should adapt to the ill child, if necessary. In other cases, the child is placed in a class with other disabled students.

INITIAL EVALUATION FOR THE IEP

When your child or adolescent is being considered for "exceptional education" (or special education or whatever they call it in your state) for the first time, expect a pretty rigorous review. Educating children outside of the regular classroom can be costly because the classes for disabled children are usually much smaller and require far closer supervision than "regular" classes. This means that it costs the school, county, or whoever pays the bill more money.

You may need to speak to the school social worker or psychologist. This person may wish to visit you in your home and talk with you and your child, as well as observe the child's behavior—and probably your behavior, too. When the school social worker came to our house, Jane was in a terrible mood and she screamed and yelled and stomped off, basically for no apparent reason. This is behavior she never exhibits when she is well! Nor did I "coach" her, as some parents are accused of doing.

The next step may be to meet with a host of professionals, what I call a "cast of thousands," and this can be quite intimidating if you're not forewarned. The principal of the school your child may attend, a guidance counselor, a therapist, if the school has one, at least one teacher, and others will probably attend. As many as ten or more people may appear at this "staffing" (jargon for a team evaluation of eligibility for a program). They will probably ask you questions and will discuss with you the problems, how long they have existed, what the doctor says, and so forth. Papers will be issued and signed.

I strongly recommend that you *not* go to such a meeting alone, nor should you go to the first IEP session alone. It can be intimidating to see grim-faced educators and others deciding your child's fate. If you don't have a spouse, take a sibling or a friend. If you can, take your doctor! (This impresses them tremendously. Of course, you will have to pay the psychiatrist or therapist for his or her time and insurance may not reimburse you for this, but it may well be worth the expense.)

Once the "team" decides that your child is eligible, then you move to the next step. If they decide your child is not eligible, appeal it. Always remember that in virtually any bureaucracy, there is an appeal process. Oftentimes people will give in to you because you wear them down. I see no problem with this tactic if you truly believe that your child needs an education outside the mainstream classroom. There may be several levels of appeal.

THE INDIVIDUALIZED EDUCATION PROGRAM (IEP)

After your child is accepted into the program, a team of teachers and administrators develops an educational plan. This plan is called an "individualized education program" or IEP. A new IEP must be drawn up each year, by federal law. As a parent, you are entitled to see the results of any tests or examinations that affect the evaluation; you can also request a copy of these documents. You are also entitled to see the child's entire school record although the school is allowed to charge you for photocopying if you want a copy.

The team will talk to you about their goals and plans for your child, which they will have written out, and you have the right to (and should) provide your own opinions and ask questions. Certainly if you don't like something, speak up! To truly advocate for your child or for your mentally ill relative of any age, you cannot be a shrinking violet—you *must* become strongly assertive. For example, in one of our IEP sessions, I noted that virtually all the goals were "social" goals, such as speaking to other people, maintaining eye contact rather than averting eyes, and so forth. But where, I wondered, was the academic information—the specific goals or tasks to be mastered in math and other subjects? I described the goals that I felt were important and they were added. Other goals that I thought were senseless, silly, or unachievable were deleted. Will the IEP group think you are a pain? Maybe. But who cares? It's important to tell them, in a polite and respectful manner, what you think. You need to be your child's advocate.

Your child may also attend these sessions and this can be difficult, particularly if the staff's comments are hard for the child to accept. Keep your child's level of coping skills in mind. Understand that if you are intimidated by or fearful of a group of adults sitting at a long table, your child may well be terrified. This doesn't mean you should never let the child attend! It may be helpful and instructive for the child. He will learn from this meeting what will be expected. This is also your child's chance to offer any comments.

Once an agreement is reached, you sign the IEP, as do all the other participants. Your child may also sign this document. And then it's over, for another year. What if you don't agree with the IEP and no matter what you say or do, the staff will not budge? Refuse to sign. Tell them that you will appeal, and do so. Consult with your child's physician and ask him to call people from this group. (Their names will be on the IEP form. Keep it!) In some cases, you may wish to consult your attorney.

Do try to be reasonable. Your child won't be educated in a palace with teachers hovering everywhere. Try to figure out whether what the school is offering you is reasonable or possible.

THE SCHOOL YEAR

As you move through the school year, you may find that your child's new program is in many ways like "regular" school, as well as different in many ways. For example, when my child entered her program in a special class, the school was using a rather complicated system of rewards and punishments, sort of like merits and demerits. The child earned so many points, and moved up a "level." As the child moved up levels, he or she would gain more privileges and prestige; for example, the child might be allowed to roam the halls freely. The school might even have a "point store," where trinkets and treasures could be purchased with points. The problem with a points system, for many neurobiologically disordered children, is that they may have disorganized thinking and may not really understand what is expected—or care. On the other hand, for less ill individuals, earning points may be a way to provide structure in their lives.

Another difference you may note is that you may receive periodic reports from a therapist or teacher at the school, discussing not only academic progress, but more predominantly, the child's behavior and perceived progress. Listen carefully to these reports, and remember that the person giving you the information has her own lens through which she views your child. Keeping that in mind, you may find that you gain a great deal of valuable and useful information.

I will add that the teachers and staff at a special school, or in a special program at a regular school, are generally highly motivated and they really do care about your child. They put up with incredible verbal and sometimes physical abuse from children and adolescents, and still they manage to rein in their emotions and behave in a professional and compassionate manner. That is my observation. Of course, I suspect that sometimes they must have to go off to a room somewhere and scream into a pillow.

GOING TO COLLEGE

Going to a local community college may be a good way for a mentally ill person to stay involved with the outside world; however, experts warn against encouraging a person who is recovering from psychosis to take a full load of courses—the strain may cause a relapse. Sending the person away to college is also inadvisable, again because the stress level is likely to be too high. Instead, have your relative take one or two courses to see if he can handle it. Perhaps later he will be able to work up to a full load if he wishes to. It's better for a mentally ill person to start slowly than to plunge into college with both feet.

The HEATH Resource Center published a booklet on college programs entitled *Adults with Psychiatric Disabilities on Campus*, which you may find helpful. For a free copy, call 800-544-3284.

17

THE INSURANCE SYSTEM

I f your relative is eligible for private insurance, as some are (because your relative is your child or spouse, for example), you can use these benefits to pay for services. This chapter covers private insurance benefits issues. Since the overwhelming majority of adults who are mentally ill are eligible for public assistance programs, this chapter also covers issues related to SSI and Social Security disability benefits.

PRIVATE INSURANCE

Often, private insurance does not play a role when you are the caregiver to a mentally ill person, because the person is an adult and is not covered under any health insurance that you or your spouse may have. However, if the person is covered, there are several issues to keep in mind.

When Benefits Are Denied and You Disagree

The insurance company will sometimes deny benefits that you believe should be provided, based on your particular plan. So what do you do? You appeal. Let's say that both you and your relative's doctor believe that your relative needs a longer hospital stay than the insurance company wishes to pay for. (And assuming your insurance upper limits have not been reached.) In such a case, both you and your relative's doctor may wish to appeal the insurance company's decision. In many cases, if the first appeal fails, you can appeal again.

Appeals do work, far more often than most people realize. It's not a surefire strategy for success, but it is a good one.

Get Details

When you talk to anyone at an insurance company, be sure to write down the date, the name of the person you spoke to, and, briefly, what you were told. Keep this telephone conversation log in a notebook. This is important, because if you have any more questions, you can request to speak to that person. Also, often when you tell someone at an insurance company that you were told such and such, you will be asked who told you this and when. With your notebook at hand, you can provide the information. It will greatly increase your credibility.

Try to get a commitment from the person as to when the problem will be resolved. Today? Next week? Next month? Then, if it is *not* resolved, call back and ask to speak to the same person. If you can't, at least you can say that "Mary Jones" said such-and-such on whatever date, which, again, gives you some credibility. Note that if you do not get satisfaction, you can use the procedure recommended in Chapter 15 (i.e., complain in writing to the person two levels up from the person who won't help you, and the other steps discussed).

Your Own Disability Insurance

Another point to keep in mind is that, as a caregiver to a person with a neurobiological disorder, you may wish to increase any disability insurance that you yourself have through an employer. This will provide you better coverage in the event that you do become ill and lack the income to support yourself and the mentally ill person.

SUPPLEMENTAL SECURITY INSURANCE (SSI)

Supplemental Security Insurance (SSI) is a payment to individuals who are U.S. citizens or legal aliens and are blind or disabled and have not worked long enough to be eligible for Social Security disability payments. In fact, they may not have worked at all. If your disabled relative is under age 18 and your family income is low, you may be eligible for an SSI payment for your child. Contact the local Social Security office to determine what the upper income levels are.

If the ill person is over age 18, she can apply for SSI on her own (although you will probably need to help with the paperwork). You can apply as early as one month before the person's 18th birthday. Generally, it takes at least several months before the application is decided on.

There are upper limits to the value of resources the person may own. For example, as of the summer of 1995, the applicant cannot have more than $2,000 of assets. (Cars and homes are usually excluded, as are life insurance policies with a face value of under $1,500.) If a person is on SSI and his financial situation changes—for example, he wins the lottery or inherits a million dollars—that information must be reported to the Social Security Administration.

Maximum benefit payments for 1995 for an individual are $458 a month, although some states may add to this amount; for example, maximum rates in Massachusetts for a disabled individual are $572.39. Cases are periodically reviewed ("redeterminations") to ensure that a disabled person is still disabled. At this time, additional medical information may be requested, as well as information on income and resources. A permanent residence is not a requirement for applying for SSI; thus, homeless people may apply. If the application is approved, the check can be sent to an organization where the person can pick it up.

Vocational rehabilitation services may be offered to the individual receiving SSI. If he refuses such services, the SSI benefit may be cut off.

To apply for SSI, your relative needs to provide the following documents to the Social Security Administration office:

- Social Security card or number;
- Birth certificate or other proof of age;
- Information about residence (if they have a home), such as mortgage or lease and name of landlord;
- Bank books, payroll statements, insurance policies, car registration, and other information on income and resources; and
- Names, addresses, and phone numbers of doctors, hospitals, and clinics that have provided treatment.

For further information, contact the Social Security Administration at 1-800-772-1213. If you have a hearing impairment, call 1-800-325-0778 between 7 A.M. and 7 P.M. on business days.

MEDICAID

Anyone who is eligible for SSI is also eligible for Medicaid, a state health insurance program that is usually run by some branch of the state social services office (formerly called the welfare department). Medicaid is invaluable to eligible recipients, because it will cover such health care costs as physician's fees, medication, laboratory tests, and necessary medical procedures. Parents who are receiving Aid to Families with Dependent Children (AFDC) also receive Medicaid. Sometimes people do not receive a monthly check, but they continue to be eligible for Medicaid alone.

Not all doctors accept Medicaid, so your relative may have to change doctors; however, if she has been seeing the same physician for years, ask that doctor to consider continuing with your relative. The answer might just be yes!

If your relative is over age 18, you should investigate the SSI and Medicaid option, unless you are independently wealthy. (Even if you are wealthy, you will be shocked to learn how quickly funds can be used up to pay for hospitalizations.) To apply for Medicaid, you need to obtain the proper forms from your local social services office. You should apply for SSI first, then Medicaid. Expect delays, long waits in the office, and plenty of confusion. Don't take it personally. If your relative is denied benefits, appeal. Many appeals succeed.

SSA DISABILITY

If your relative has been working and paying into Social Security, he may be eligible for a work-related disability and for Medicare coverage, even when he is under age 65. Medicare is different from Medicaid and one difference is that it is federally administered. The ill person may also be eligible based on a deceased parent's earnings. Rules are constantly changing. Contact the Social Security office in your area for further information.

STATE SOCIAL SERVICES—"WELFARE"

As the caregiver to a mentally ill person, you will probably encounter the state social services system. In an ideal world, the workers would be compassionate and kind and you wouldn't have to wait long for information. In reality, you and your relative will probably wait in crowded, dirty rooms full of screaming children and frustrated-looking adults. When your name is finally called, you will go to the desk of a worker who will ask many questions and will want various documents, such as a birth certificate. It's a good idea to ask ahead of time what information you should bring, but the person you call may forget one or two needed items. If that is so, you will have to come back later and probably go through the whole thing again.

The social services system is a huge bureaucracy with many rules, some of which may seem idiotic to you; they probably seem idiotic to the people who work in the system, as well. But rules must be followed! Most middle-class people—okay, most *people*—find applying a torturous and demeaning process. However, this is what you need to go through to obtain Medicaid or other services that your relative may need.

If the above description sounds too negative, let me add that I have worked in a social services office, and as a private citizen I have helped people apply for assistance. If your experience is positive, great! This is one area where I would like to be wrong.

THE MEDICAID CARD

One problem that some caregivers have faced is that for some reason, the relative's Medicaid card has not arrived, although they have been assured by the social services office that their relative has been approved. Some pharmacies have a direct link to the state social service offices and can verify, by computer, that your relative is "in the system." As long as your relative can provide some simple proof of identity, you can then obtain the necessary medication. If it's medical services you need, ask the social worker to issue a special letter authorizing services until the Medicaid card does arrive, and give that letter to the doctor. (Make copies of it first!)

18

THE CRIMINAL JUSTICE AND SUBSTANCE ABUSE SYSTEMS

In addition to hospitals and medical bureaucracies, insurance companies and educational systems, there are other systems that you may encounter as a caregiver to a mentally ill person. Sadly, large numbers of inmates in jails and prisons are mentally ill, and many are there for relatively minor offenses. As a result, the criminal justice system is one area that I'll discuss briefly.

Another problem for many mentally ill people is substance abuse, particularly abuse of alcohol or illegal drugs. Experts don't know whether mentally ill people abuse drugs and alcohol in an effort to self-medicate or in an effort to escape their problems—or both. Some experts believe that substance abuse can bring out mental illness in a vulnerable, but previously sane, person. Most psychiatrists recommend that people with neurobiological disorders refrain from using alcohol altogether. (And, of course, they should not use illegal drugs.) If you suspect that your relative is abusing drugs or alcohol, be certain to notify the psychiatrist.

THE CRIMINAL JUSTICE SYSTEM

If a person can't understand what the "rules" are or doesn't think they apply to him, he may well not comply with them. This is the problem that mentally ill people have and, as a result, many are incarcerated for relatively minor crimes such as vandalism or trespassing. The National Alliance for the Mentally Ill (NAMI) offers a booklet entitled *A Guide to Mental Illness and the Criminal Justice System: A Systems Guide for Families and Consumers* for families whose relatives may be (or have been) involved with the criminal justice system. The cost is $5.

Although her son has yet to be hospitalized for writing threatening letters to important public officials, one mother is afraid that day will come. She says she knows the Secret Service is aware of her son because he has sent letters threatening the President. She tries to talk him out of writing these letters or to intercept them before they are sent—but so far, it's been impossible to catch them all. Such problems can be heartbreaking for families.

Holly Cmiel speaks poignantly of being in court with her son and five psychiatrists who were willing to attest that her son was mentally ill and should be placed in the state hospital. In addition, the attorney and public defender agreed that her son desperately needed hospitalization. So she thought that at long last, her son would finally get the help he so desperately needed. She was wrong.

"My son was standing in front of the judge, and he had to be held up by two sheriffs. He had holes in his shoes and terrible, filthy clothes." The judge declared him mentally competent. Cmiel continues, "The whole courtroom was snickering and laughing. In the courtroom with me were sitting drug addicts and prostitutes and these people were laughing at my son who was sick and that this judge would release him to the streets again."

This was an unfortunate situation, but Cmiel ultimately did ensure that her son received treatment—after a courageous fight to get him there.

Required Treatment for Released Prisoners

Law professor Samuel Jan Brakel believes that there is a trend toward requiring mentally ill people who are released from jail or prison to take medication, as a condition of either probation or parole. "The mood to punish offenders is, I believe, matched by a mood to assert greater authority over the lives of people who can't manage their mental illness," says Brakel. Another situation in which medication may be mandated, says Brakel, is "as a condition of discharge of people acquitted of a crime by reason of insanity after they have served a stint in a hospital for forensic patients. There is even evidence that this trend is being extended to discharges from civil hospitals."

He continues,

> People who have been charged with a crime, but found unfit to stand trial or found not guilty by reason of insanity after a trial, as well as those convicted of crime (i.e., those detained in institutions like prisons or "forensic" mental hospitals) have lesser rights to refuse treatment than civil patients. That is to say, their objections to medication can be overridden by relatively efficient medical/administrative decisions (as opposed to full judicial process) so long as it can be shown the treatment is in their best medical interest and/or comports with the institution's security needs. According to the prevailing law, the issue of the competency of these criminal or forensic patients to decide on their treatment need not be considered.

THE SUBSTANCE ABUSE SYSTEM

In many cases, people with neurobiological illness turn to alcohol or illegal substances. This is a serious problem, not only in its own right, but also because drugs or alcohol can impair the effect of psychiatric medication. Some experts believe that the more efficacious the psychiatric medication, the greater the risk that substance abuse could impair the person. And of course, the person who is using illegal drugs may be charged and imprisoned if caught.

Yet, people who are severely mentally ill are at high risk for becoming substance abusers; as many as half of this population do become substance abusers. As a result, experts recommend that people with severe mental illness totally abstain from alcohol or other drugs. Experts differ on why some people have a "dual diagnosis" of substance abuse and mental illness. Some believe that the mentally ill person who uses illegal drugs or alcohol is trying to diminish or wipe out symptoms. Others believe that alcohol or drug abuse can trigger psychotic behavior in vulnerable people.

One big problem today is that many treatment centers for people with drug or alcohol abuse problems won't accept mentally ill patients. And the psychiatric hospitals don't want to deal with drug or alcohol abusers. Another problem is that if a person with a dual diagnosis is placed in one of these institutions, her treatment will depend on the site; for example, if she is placed in a psychiatric facility, the staff may concentrate on the mental illness rather than providing substance abuse treatment. Conversely, if the person is placed in a drug treatment center, the importance of drug treatment is paramount, rather than the treatment of psychiatric problems. In some cases, the drug treatment center may even be opposed to psychiatric medications.

What can you do about the problem of dual diagnoses, particularly in a family member? Experts say that recognizing substance abuse as a common problem among mentally ill people is a good start. So don't ignore indications of alcohol or drug abuse. Also, families can advocate for their relatives if and when institutional treatment is required. They can argue in favor of educating the existing staff, or adding staff members who can provide assistance to both staff and the person with a dual diagnosis.

Alchohol Abuse and Psychiatric Medications

One difficulty associated with obtaining treatment for ill people with an alcohol abuse problem is that some programs and some support groups conclude that all medications are bad. Yet, a psychotic person may need psychiatric medications more than ever while trying to combat a problem with alcohol abuse.

Says Dr. Bertram Warren, a psychiatrist in Plainfield, New Jersey, "I see recovering alcoholics—and these folks tend to have psychiatric illnesses underneath. They may have panic disorder or depression or other illnesses and they need to be on psychiatric medications. But some of them go to AA [Alcoholics Anonymous] meetings where the group is opposed to all medication. So I tell them to find a different AA meeting—because there are AA meetings and there are AA meetings—some are much more understanding."

CONCLUSION

It's difficult to be the caregiver of a person with a serious neurobiological disorder, and even when people are kind, it can be grating. You might have heard, for example, "I could never handle that! But you are a very strong person." Or the ever-popular, "God gives us only burdens that we can handle," or some variation of that religious homily—invariably said on a day when you feel like you want to run around screaming.

My view is that our relatives don't deserve to be mentally ill and we don't deserve the responsiblity of caregiving. I do not personally believe that divine powers use mental illness to test our mettle or punish us. Mental illness happens. It happens in the best of families, to the worst of families, and to the average family—whatever that is today. We who care for our ill relatives do it because we love them and because we believe, in most cases, that the alternatives are unacceptable. Sometimes we are wrong and we find that our relative would be more functional in a different environment. Most of the time, though, we are probably right because of the serious dearth of adequate places for people with neurobiological disorders to live.

My hope is that after reading this book, you will realize how very important you are to your ill relative and that you will appreciate yourself. If you have been ashamed or embarrassed about your relative's "problem," I hope you will lay down that burden.

There are no quick fixes or easy answers to providing caregiving for our relatives. I have offered some strategies and tactics that I hope will work for you. And I have tried to offer you a "cheerleading" mentality to energize you and give you the hope you need. So many of my interviewees urged me to tell you that you must *never* give up hope. I agree. As a result, I would like to leave you with this quotation from Prime Minister Sir Winston Churchill to students at Harrow School, in the dark days of World War II. I think it combines the qualities of hope and strength that you will marshal as a caregiver: "Never give in, never give in, never, never, never, never—in nothing, great or small, large or petty, never give in except to convictions of honor and good sense."

And never forget that you are not alone in dealing with this problem. There is help, empathy, and caring out there for you and for your relative.

PART FOUR

APPENDIXES

IMPORTANT TOLL-FREE NUMBERS

Alzheimer's Disease and Related Disorders Association
  800-621-0379

Americans with Disabilities Act (ADA)
  ADA Publications
  800-669-3362

ADA Information Hotline
  800-949-4232

NAMI (National Alliance for the Mentally Ill) Helpline
  800-950-NAMI

National Rehabilitation Information
  800-346-2742

Social Security Administration (SSA)
  800-SSA-1213

Vocational Research Institute
  800-874-5387

RECOMMENDED BOOKS

The Boy Who Couldn't Stop Washing: The Experience and Treatment of Obsessive-Compulsive Disorder by Judith L. Rapoport. Published by Dutton, New York, 1990. This book offers anecdotal information and a clear explanation of this disorder.

The Encyclopedia of Schizophrenia and the Psychotic Disorders by Richard Noll, M.A. Published by Facts on File, Inc., New York, 1992. A valuable A-Z reference book that explains many aspects of mental illness. It's probably available in your local library.

Grieving Mental Illness: A Guide for Patients and Caregivers by Virginia Lafond. Published by University of Toronto Press, Toronto, Canada, 1994. Covers the anger, sadness, denial, and other issues involved in coping with mental illness. Written by someone who has been there.

Homes That Help: Advice from Caregivers for Creating a Supportive Home by Richard V. Olsen, Ph.D.; Ezara Ehrenkrantz, F.A.I.A; and Barbara Hutchings, M. ARCH. Published by New Jersey Institute of Technology, Newark, New Jersey, 1990. Many practical and helpful hints for caregivers of older people with Alzheimer's or other dementias.

Planning for the Future: Providing a Meaningful Life for a Child with a Disability After Your Death by L. Mark Russell, J.D.; Arnold E. Grant, J.D.; Suzanne M. Joseph, C.F.P.; Richard W. Fee, M.Ed., M.A. Published by American Publishing Company, P.O. Box 988, Evanston, IL 60204-0988, 1994. This is a helpful and informative guide.

Madness in the Streets: How Psychiatry and the Law Abandoned the Mentally Ill by Rael Jean Isaac and Virginia C. Armat. Published by The Free Press, 1990. A powerful and detailed account of the true story of our homeless.

Stigma and Mental Illness, edited by Paul Jay Fink, M.D. and Allan Tasman, M.D. Published by American Psychiatric Press, Washington, D.C., 1992. A fascinating book for anyone who wants to understand where the stigma against mental illness came from and who is affected.

Surviving Schizophrenia: A Manual for Families, Consumers and Providers by E. Fuller Torrey, M.D. Published by Harper Perennial, New York, 1995. This is a classic and should be required reading for caregivers of people with schizophrenia as well as extended family members and all providers of services to people with this illness.

You Mean I Don't Have to Feel This Way? New Help for Depression, Anxiety, and Addiction by Colette Dowling. Published by Charles Scribner's Sons, 1991. The author draws on personal experiences within her family and combines this background with information and advice from experts. An intriguing book.

POLICE CRISIS INFORMATION FORM

Please take this person to _____ Hospital.

Important! This person is NOT a criminal. She/he has a mental illness. Please treat with compassion and dignity. Thank you.

Name _____ Age _____

Name of Doctor_____

Address _____ Doctor's Phone _____

_____ Hospital _____

Tel. _____ Birthdate _____

Current Medications & Dose _____

Social Security No._____ Suicidal _____ Violent _____

Med. Ins. (If any) _____

Date of Last Hosp _____ How Long _____

SSI? _____ SSDI? _____ Other _____ Allergies? _____

Eye color _____ Hair color _____ High Blood Pressure _____

Race _____

Name of Outpatient Program _____

Blood type ____ Glasses? _____ Name of Social Worker _____

Height _____ Weight _____ Emergency Contact Person _____

Identifying Marks _____ Rel. to Patient _____

Military/VA Status _____ Contact Person Address _____

Primary Diagnosis _____ _____

Secondary Diagnosis_____ Day Phone _____

_____ Work Phone _____

Other Information _____

Source: Adapted from a form published in the September/October 1992 issue of *The Best of the AMI/FAMI Reporter*, published by the Friends and Advocates of the Mentally Ill, Inc., New York, New York.

APPENDIX D

EXAMPLE OF AUTHORIZATION TO RELEASE INFORMATION

Permission is hereby given to _____ to release information, including psychiatric, psychological, drug and alcohol information contained in the medical records of

_____   _____

Full Name of Patient   Patient's Birthdate

1. This release shall comply with federal regulations (42 CFR part 2) and applicable state laws.

2. Information released to the above may not be redisclosed without further authorization by signature.

3. This authorization will expire from 60 days of the date of signature or upon completion of treatment, whichever is later. It may be revoked by the patient/ representative at any time.

4. The patient/representative has been offered the opportunity to discuss the advantages and disadvantages of releasing the information.

5. This authorization is voluntarily given.

Names of persons, agencies or organization to which information may be released.

Name_____

Address_____

Specific Information to Be Released_____

Dates of Treatment for Which Information Is Requested

_____

_____   _____   _____   _____

Signature of Patient/Representative   Date   Signature of Witness   Date

NATIONAL ALLIANCE FOR THE MENTALLY ILL (NAMI) STATE AFFILIATE LIST

National Headquarters

National Alliance for the Mentally Ill (NAMI)
200 N. Glebe Rd.
Arlington, VA 22203-3754
800-950-NAMI

Or call your state affiliate to find a local chapter near you.

Alabama AMI
6900 6th Avenue South, Suite B
Birmingham, AL 35212-1902
Phone: (205)833-8336
FAX: (205)833-8336(ND)

Alaska AMI
110 W. 15th Ave., Suite B
Anchorage, AK 99501
Phone: (907)277-1300
FAX: (907)277-1400

Arizona AMI (AAMI)
2441 E. Fillmore St
Phoenix, AZ 85008-6033
Phone: (602)244-8166
FAX: (602)220-0934

Arkansas AMI–Help and Hope, Inc
4313 W. Markham St.
Hendrix Hall, Room 233
Little Rock, AR 72205-4096
Phone: (501)661-1548
FAX: (501)664-0264

California AMI
1111 Howe Ave., Suite 475
Sacramento, CA 95825-8541
Phone: (916)567-0163
FAX: (916)567-1757

Colorado AMI
1100 Fillmore St.
Denver, CO 80206-3334
Phone: (303)321-3104
FAX: (303)321-0912 (ND)

Connecticut AMI
151 New Park Ave
Hartford, CT 06106
Phone: (203)586-2319
FAX: (203)586-7121

AMI DC Threshold
422 8th St. SE
Washington, DC 20003-2832
Phone: (202)546-0646
FAX: (202)546-6817

AMID (AMI Delaware)
2500 W. 4th St.
4th St. Plaza, Suite 12
Wilmington, DE 19805
Phone: (302)427-0787
FAX: (302)427-2075

Florida AMI
304 N. Meridian St., Suite 2
Tallahassee, FL 32301
Phone: (904)222-3400
FAX: (904)222-3400 (ND)

Georgia AMI
1256 Briarcliff Rd. NE, Room 412-S
Atlanta, GA 30306-2636
Phone: (404)894-8860
FAX: (404)894-8862

Hawaii State AMI
1126 12th Ave., Suite 205
Honolulu, HI 96816-3714
Phone: (808)737-2778
FAX: (808)734-3477

Idaho AMI
331 N. Allumbaugh St.
Boise, ID 83704-9208
Phone: (208)376-2143

AMI Illinois State Coalition
730 East Vine St., Room 209
Springfield, IL 62703
Phone: (217)522-1403
FAX: (217)522-3598

Indiana AMI
P.O. Box 22697
Indianapolis, IN 46222-0697
Phone: (317)236-0056
FAX: (317)236-8166

AMI of Iowa
5911 Meredith Dr., Suite C-1
Des Moines, IA 50322-1903
Phone: (515)254-0417
FAX: (515)254-1103

Kansas AMI
112 S.W. 6th
P.O. Box 675
Topeka, KS 66601-0675
Phone: (913)233-0755
FAX: (913)233-4804

Kentucky AMI
10510 LaGrange Rd., Bldg. 103
Louisville, KY 40223-1228
Phone: (502)245-5284
FAX: (502)245-5287

Louisiana AMI
P.O. Box 2547
Baton Rouge, LA 70821-2547
Phone: (504)343-6928
FAX: (504)388-9133

AMI-ME (AMI-Maine)
P.O. Box 222
Augusta, ME 04332-0222
Phone: (207)622-5767
FAX: (207)622-5767 (ND)

AMI of Maryland, Inc.
711 W. 40th St., Suite 451
Baltimore, MD 21211
Phone: (410)467-7100
(800)467-0075
FAX: (410)467-7195

AMI of Massachusetts, Inc.
295 Devonshire St.
Boston, MA 02210-1625
Phone: (617)426-2299
FAX: (617)426-0088

AMI of Michigan
921 N. Washington
Lansing, MI 48906
Phone: (517)485-4049
FAX: (517)485-2333

AMI of Minnesota, Inc.
970 Raymond Ave., Suite 105
St. Paul, MN 55114-1146
Phone: (612)645-2948
FAX: (612)645-7379

Mississippi AMI
P.O. Box 5322
Brandon, MS 39047
Phone: (601)992-1227
FAX: (601)992-2791

Missouri Coalition of AMI
204 E. High St.
Jefferson City, MO 65101-3260
Phone: (314)634-7727
(800)374-2138
FAX: (314)634-7727 (ND)

MONAMI (Montana AMI)
P.O. Box 1021
Helena, MT 59624
Phone: (406)443-7871
FAX: (406)443-1592

Nebraska AMI
814 Lyncrest Dr.
Lincoln, NE 68510-4022
Phone: (402)489-6239

AMI of Nevada
1027 S. Rainbow Blvd., Suite 172
Las Vegas, NV 89128
Phone: (702)254-2666
FAX: (702)363-5485

AMI of New Hampshire
10 Ferry St., Unit 314
Concord, NH 03301-5004
Phone: (603)225-5359
FAX: (603)228-8848

New Jersey AMI
200 W. State St., 3rd Floor
Trenton, NJ 08608-1102
Phone: (609)695-4554
FAX: (609)695-0908

AMI New Mexico
1720 Louisiana Blvd. NE, Suite 214
Albuquerque, NM 87110
Phone: (505)254-0643
FAX: (505)254-0674

AMI-NYS (New York State)
260 Washington Ave.
Albany, NY 12210-1312
Phone: (518)462-2000
(800)950-3228
FAX: (518)426-0504

North Carolina AMI
4904 Waters Edge Dr., Suite 152
Raleigh, NC 27606
Phone: (919)851-0063
FAX: (919)851-5989

North Dakota AMI
401 S. Main
Minot, ND 58701
Phone: (701)852-5324
FAX: (701)852-1742

AMI of Ohio
979 S. High St.
Columbus, OH 43206-2525
Phone: (614)444-2646
(800)686-2646
FAX: (614)445-6503

Oklahoma AMI
1140 N. Hudson Ave.
Oklahoma City, OK 73103-3906
Phone: (800)583-1264
FAX: (405)239-6264

Oregon AMI
161 High St. SE, Suite 212
Salem, OR 97301-3610
Phone: (503)370-7774
FAX: (503)370-9452

AMI of Pennsylvania
2149 N. 2nd St.
Harrisburg, PA 17110-1005
Phone: (717)238-1514
FAX: (717)238-4390

AMI of Rhode Island
P.O. Box 28411
Providence, RI 02908-0411
Phone: (401)464-3060
FAX: (401)464-1686

South Dakota AMI
P.O. Box 221
Brookings, SD 57006
Phone: (605)697-7210
(800)551-2531
FAX: (605)692-6132

South Carolina AMI
P.O. Box 2538
Columbia, SC 29202-2538
Phone: (803)779-7849
FAX: (803)779-7849 (ND)

Tennessee AMI
1900 N. Winston Rd., Suite 511
Knoxville, TN 37919
Phone: (615)531-8264
FAX: (615)691-0103

Texas AMI (TEXAMI)
1000 E. 7th St., Suite 208
Austin, TX 78702-3257
Phone: (512)474-2225
FAX: (512)320-8887

Utah AMI
P.O. Box 58047
Salt Lake City, UT 84158-0047
Phone: (801)584-2023
FAX: (801)582-8471

AMI of Vermont
230 Main St., Room 203
Brattleboro, VT 05301-2840
Phone: (802)257-5546
(800)639-6480
FAX: (802)257-5886

Virginia AMI
P.O. Box 1903
Richmond, VA 23215-1903
Phone: (804)225-8264
(800)484-7753 + VAMI(8264)
FAX: (804)643-3632

AMI of Washington State
4305 Lacey Blvd. SE, Suite 11
Lacey, WA 98503-5718
Phone: (206)438-0211
FAX: (206)493-0431

West Virginia AMI
P.O. Box 2706
Charleston, WV 25330-2706
Phone: (304)342-0497
FAX: (304)342-0499

AMI of Wisconsin, Inc.
1410 Northport Dr.
Madison, WI 53704-2041
Phone: (608)242-7223
FAX: (608)242-7225

Wyoming AMI (WYAMI)
P.O. Box 391
Casper, WY 82602
Phone: (307)234-6246

IMPORTANT NATIONAL ORGANIZATIONS

Alzheimer's Disease and Related
   Disorders Association
919 N. Michigan Ave., Suite 1000
Chicago, IL 60611-1676
312-335-8700
800-272-3900

American Association for Partial
Hospitalization, Inc.
901 N. Washington, #600
Alexandria, VA 22314
703-836-2274

American Hospital Association
840 Lake Shore Dr.
Chicago, IL 60611
312-280-6000

American Psychiatric Association
1400 K St. NW
Washington, DC 20002
202-336-5500

American Psychological Association
750 First St. NW
Washington, DC 20002
202-336-5500

Anxiety Disorders Association of
   America
6000 Executive Blvd., Suite 513
Rockville, MD 20850
301-231-9350

Autism Services Center
P.O. Box 507
Huntington, WV 25710-0507
304-525-8014

Autism Society of America
7910 Woodmont Ave., Suite 655
Bethesda, MD 20814
301-657-0881

Children and Adults with Attention
   Deficit Disorders (CH.A.D.D.)
1859 N. Pine Island Rd., Suite 185
Plantation, FL 33322
305-587-3700

Homeless and Missing Persons Network
National Alliance for Mentally Ill
1239 C Russell Parkway, Suite 20
Warner Robbins, GA 31088
912-328-3555

Mental Illness Foundation
420 Lexington Ave., Suite 2104
New York, NY 10170
212-682-4699

National Alliance for the Mentally Ill
200 N. Glebe Rd., Suite 1015
Arlington, VA 22203-3754
Helpline: 800-950-NAMI
Regular line: 703-524-7600

National Alliance for Research on
   Schizophrenia & Depression
   (NARSAD)
60 Cutter Mill Rd., Suite. 200
Great Neck, NY 11021
516-829-0091

National Association of Social Workers
750 First St. NE
Washington, DC 20002
202-408-8600

National Coalition for the Mentally Ill in
    the Criminal Justice System
600 Stewart St., Suite 520
Seattle, WA 98101-1217
206-628-7021

National Crisis Prevention Institute
3315K N. 124th St.
Brookfield, WI 53005
414-783-5787
800-558-8976

National Depressive and Manic
    Depressive Association
730 N. Franklin St., Suite 501
Chicago, IL 60610-3526
800-82-NDMDA

National Foundation for Depressive
    Illness
P.O. Box 2257
New York, NY 10116
212-268-4260

National Institute for Mental Health
    (NIMH)
5600 Fishers Lane, Room 7C-02
Rockville, MD 20857
301-443-4513

National Mental Health Association
1021 Prince St.
Alexandria, VA 22314-2971
703-684-7722

National Mental Health Consumers
    Association Self-Help Clearinghouse
311 South Juniper St., Suite 1000
Philadelphia, PA 19107
800-553-4539

Obsessive Compulsive Foundation
P.O. Box 9573
New Haven, CT 06535
203-772-0565

Parent Advocacy Coalition for
    Educational Rights (PACER) Center
4826 Chicago Ave. South
Minneapolis, MN 55417
612-827-2966

Tourette Syndrome Association
100 TechneCenter Drive
Park 50 TechneCenter, Suite 116
Milford, OH 45150-2713
513-831-2976

APPENDIX G

SELF-HELP CLEARINGHOUSES, BY STATE

Arizona
The Rainy Day People
P.O. Box 472
Scottsdale, AZ 85252
602-840-1029

California
California Self-Help Center
U.C.L.A.
405 Hildgard Ave.
Los Angeles, CA 90024
800-222-LINK
213-825-1799

Sacramento Self-Help Clearinghouse
Mental Health Association of
    Sacramento
5370 Elvos Ave., Suite B
Sacramento, CA 95819

San Francisco Self-Help Clearinghouse
Mental Health Association
2398 Pine St.
San Francisco, CA 94115

Connecticut
Self-Help Mutual Support Network
    Consultation Center
19 Howe St.
New Haven, CT 06511
203-789-7645

District of Columbia
Family Stress Services of D.C.
2001 O St. NW, Suite 6
Washington, DC 20036
202-628-FACT

Florida
Hotline Information Referral
P.O. Box 13087
St. Petersburg, FL 33733
813-531-4664

Illinois
Self-Help Center
405 State St.
Champaign, IL 61820
217-352-0099

Indiana
Information and Referral Network
1828 N. Meridian St.
Indianapolis, IN 46202
317-921-1305

Iowa
Iowa Self-Help Clearinghouse
33 N. 12th St.
P.O. Box 1151
Fort Dodge, IA 50501
515-576-5870

Kansas
Kansas Self-Help Network
Wichita State University
Campus Box 34
Wichita, KS 67208-1595
316-689-3170

Massachusetts
Clearinghouse of Mutual Self-Help
  Groups
Massachusetts Cooperative Extension
University of Massachusetts
113 Skinner Hall
Amherst, MA 01003
413-545-2313

Michigan
Michigan Self-Help Clearinghouse
Michigan Protection & Advocacy
  Service
109 W. Michigan Ave., Suite 900
Lansing, MI 48933
517-484-7373
800-752-5858 (MI only)

Minnesota
Minnesota Mutual Help Resource Center
Wilder Foundation Community Care
  Unit
919 LaFond Ave.
St. Paul, MN 55104
612-242-4060

Missouri
Mental Health Association of St. Louis
3617 Shaw Blvd.
St. Louis, MO 63110
314-773-1399

Nebraska
Self-Help Information Services
1601 Euclid Ave.
Lincoln, NE 68502
402-476-9668

New Hampshire
New Hampshire Self-Help
  Clearinghouse
Office of Public Education
Division of Mental Health &
  Developmental Services
105 Pleasant St.
State Office Park South
Concord, NH 03301
603-271-5060

New Jersey
New Jersey Self-Help Clearinghouse
St. Clare's Riverside Medical Center
Pocono Rd.
Denville, NJ 07834
201-625-9565
800-367-6274 (NJ only)

New York
New York State Self-Help Clearinghouse
NY Council on Children and Families
Empire State Plaza Tower 2
Albany, NY 12224
518-474-6293

North Carolina
Supportworks
1012 Kings Drive, Suite 923
Charlotte, NC 28283
704-331-9500

Ohio
Ohio Self-Help Clearinghouse
Family Service Association
184 Salem Ave.
Dayton, OH 45406
513-222-9481

Oregon
Northwest Regional Self-Help
  Clearinghouse
718 W. Burnside Ave.
Portland, OR 97209
503-222-5555

Pennsylvania
Self-Help Information & Networking
Exchange
Voluntary Action Center of Northeast
Pennsylvania
225 N. Washington Ave.
Park Plaza, Lower Level
Scranton, PA 18503
717-961-1234

Rhode Island
Support Group Helpline
Rhode Island Department of Health
Cannon Building, Davis St.
Providence, RI 09208
401-277-2223

South Carolina
The Support Group Network
Lexington Medical Center
2720 Sunset Blvd.
West Columbia, SC 29169
803-791-9227

Tennessee
Support Group Clearinghouse
Mental Health Association of Knox
County
6712 Kingston Pike, Suite 203
Knoxville, TN 37919
615-584-6736

Texas
Greater San Antonio Self-Help
Clearinghouse
Mental Health Association
1407 N. Main
San Antonio, TX 78212
512-222-1571

Vermont
Vermont Self-Help Clearinghouse
P.O. Box 829
Montpelier, VT 05602
802-229-5724

Virginia
Greater Virginia Self-Help Coalition
Mental Health Association of Northern
Virginia
100 N. Washington St., Suite 232
Falls Church, VA 22046

Washington
Crisis Clinic
P.O. Box 2463
Olympia, WA 98507
800-627-2211

Wisconsin
Health and Human Services Outreach
University of Wisconsin-Madison
610 Langdon St.
414 Lowell Hall
Madison, WI 53706
608-263-4432

PLAN PROGRAMS

Special programs to ensure services are provided to your ill relative after your incapacity or death are listed here (see Chapter 14).

Arizona
PLAN in development stage
Contact: Frances Peterson, c/o AAMI
2441 East Fillmore
Phoenix, AZ 85008
602-244-8166

California
Proxy Parent Services Foundation
1336 Wilshire Blvd., 2nd Fl.
Los Angeles, CA 90017
213-413-1130

Connecticut
PLAN in development stage
Contact: Ilene Kaplan, President
22 Cottonwood Ave.
Avon, CT 06001
203-673-6695

Florida
PLAN in development stage
Contact: Jean Haydu Harris
875 East Camino Real
Boca Raton, FL 33432
407-558-0627

Georgia
PLAN of Georgia
55 Elizabeth Church Rd.
Marietta, GA 30064

Illinois
PACT, Inc.
340 West Butterfield Rd.
Elmhurst, IL 60126

Indiana
ARC of Indiana
22 East Washington St., Suite 210
Indianapolis, IN 46204
317-632-4387

Maryland
PLAN of Maryland-DC, Inc.
912 Thayer Ave.
Silver Spring, MD 20910
301-229-8269

New Hampshire
PLAN in development stage
Contact: Ed Broad
413 Blodget St.
Manchester, NH 03104
603-623-5191

New Jersey
PLAN of New Jersey
1275 Bound Brook Rd., Suite 1
Middlesex, NJ 08846
908-563-0300

New York
PLAN of New York
432 Park Avenue South
Suite 1201
New York, NY 10016
212-545-7063

North Carolina
Life Plan Trust, Inc.
P.O. Box 20545
Raleigh, NC 27619
919-782-4632

Ohio
PLAN of Northeast Ohio
3130 Mayfield Rd., Suite GW112
Cleveland Heights, OH 44118
216-321-3611

Pennsylvania
PLAN of Pennsylvania
110 West Lancaster Ave.
Wayne, PA 19087
215-687-4036

Texas
PLAN of North Texas
4040 Highgrove Dr.
Executive Tower, Suite 723
Dallas, TX 75220
214-350-3478

Virginia
Personal Support Network
100 North Washington St., Suite 234
Falls Church, VA 22042
703-532-3303

Washington
PLAN in development stage
Contact: Ted Chaney
Washington AMI
24226 9th Ave. South
Des Moines, WA 98198

Note: If there is no PLAN program in
your state, contact your state NAMI
office. There may be a similar program
that would suit your needs.

APPENDIX I
STATE MENTAL HEALTH OFFICES*

Alabama
Department of Mental Health & Mental
 Retardation
200 Interstate Park
Montgomery, AL 36109
205-271-9207

Alaska
Mental Health & Developmental
Disabilities Division
P.O. Box 110620
Juneau, AK 99811
907-465-3370

California
Department of Mental Health
1600 9th St.
Sacramento, CA 95814
916-654-2309

Connecticut
Department of Mental Health
90 Washington St.
Hartford, CT 06106
203-566-3869

Delaware
Division of Alcoholism, Drug Abuse &
 Mental Health
1901 N. Du Pont Highway
New Castle, DE 19720
302-577-4461

District of Columbia
Mental Health Services
Department of Human Services
2700 M.L. King Jr. Ave, SE
Washington, DC 20032
202-673-7166

Florida
Alcohol, Drug Abuse & Mental Health
Department of Health & Rehabilitative
 Services
1317 Winewood Blvd.
Bldg. 6, Rm. 183
Tallahassee, FL 32399
904-488-8304

Georgia
Department of Mental Health, Mental
Retardation & Substance Abuse
2 Peachtree St., 4th Fl.
Atlanta, GA 30303
404-657-2250

Hawaii
Behavioral Health Services
 Administration
Department of Health
1250 Punchbowl St.
Honolulu, HI 96813
808-586-4434

Idaho
Bureau of Mental Health
Department of Health & Welfare
450 W. State St.
Boise, ID 83720
208-334-6500

*Some states do not list mental health
offices

207

Illinois
Department of Mental Health &
    Developmental Disabilities
401 Stratton Bldg.
Springfield, IL 62706
217-782-0009

Indiana
Division of Mental Health & Addictions
402 W. Washington St.
Indianapolis, IN 46204
317-232-7845

Iowa
Department of Human Services
Hoover State Office Bldg.
Des Moines, IA 50319
515-282-6360

Kansas
Mental Health & Retardation
Department of Social & Rehabilitation
    Services
Docking Off. Bldg., 5th Floor
Topeka, KS 66612
913-296-3773

Kentucky
Mental Health & Retardation Services
275 E. Main St.
Frankfort, KY 40621
502-564-4527

Louisiana
Office of Human Services
Department of Health & Hospitals
P.O. Box 629
Baton Rouge, LA 70821
504-342-6717

Maine
Department of Mental Health & Mental
Retardation
State House Station #40
Augusta, ME 04333
207-287-4223

Maryland
Mental Hygiene
Public Health Services
201 W. Preston St., Rm. 416A
Baltimore, MD 21201
301-225-6611

Massachusetts
Department of Mental Health
Executive Office of Human Services
25 Staniford St.
Boston, MA 02114
617-727-5500

Michigan
Department of Mental Health
300 S. Walnut, 6th Floor
Lansing, MI 48913
517-373-3500

Minnesota
Community Mental Health & Social
    Services Administration
Department of Human Services
444 Lafayette Rd.
St. Paul, MN 55155
612-296-2710

Mississippi
Department of Mental Health
1101 Robert E. Lee Bldg.
Jackson, MS 39201
601-359-1288

Missouri
Department of Mental Health
1706 E. Elm
P.O. Box 687
Jefferson City, MO 65102
314-751-3070

Montana
Mental Health Divison
Department of Institutions
1539 11th Ave.
Helena, MT 59620
406-444-3969

Nebraska
Office of Community Mental Health
Department of Public Institutions
P.O. Box 94728
Lincoln, NE 68509
402-471-2851

Nevada
Mental Hygiene & Mental Retardation
Department of Human Resources
505 E. King St., Rm. 403
Carson City, NV 89710
702-687-5943

New Hampshire
Division of Mental Health &
    Developmental Services
105 Pleasant St.
Concord, NH 03301
603-271-5007

New Jersey
Divison of Mental Health & Hospitals
Department of Human Services
Capitol Ctr., CN 727
Trenton, NJ 08625
609-777-0700

New Mexico
Division of Mental Health
Department of Health
P.O. Box 26110
Santa Fe, NM 87502
505-827-2644

New York
Office of Mental Health
44 Holland Ave.
Albany, NY 12229
518-474-4403

North Carolina
Mental Health, Retardation, & Substance
    Abuse
Department of Human Resources
325 N. Salisbury St.
Raleigh, NC 27603
919-733-7011

North Dakota
Mental Health Divison
Department of Human Services
600 E. Boulevard Ave.
Bismarck, ND 58505
701-224-2766

Ohio
Department of Mental Health
30 E. Broad St, 8th Fl.
Columbus, OH 43266
614-466-2337

Oklahoma
Department of Mental Health &
    Substance Abuse Services
P.O. Box 53277
Oklahoma City, OK 73152
405-271-8644

Oregon
Mental Health & Developmental
    Disabilities Services Div.
2575 Bitter St., NE
Salem, OR 97310
503-378-2671

Pennsylvania
Mental Health
Department of Public Welfare
Health & Welfare Bldg., Rm. 502
Harrisburg, PA 17120
717-787-6443

Rhode Island
Department of Mental Health,
  Retardation & Hospitals
600 New London Ave.
Cranston, RI 02920
401-464-3201

South Carolina
Department of Disabilities & Special
  Needs
P.O. Box 4706
Columbia, SC 29240
803-737-6444

South Dakota
Division of Mental Health
Department of Human Services
500 E. Capitol Ave.
Pierre, SD 57501
605-773-5990

Tennessee
Department of Mental Health & Mental
  Retardation
706 Church St., Suite 600
Nashville, TN 37243
615-741-3107

Texas
Department of Mental Health & Mental
  Retardation
P.O. Box 12668, Capitol Station
Austin, TX 78711
512-465-4588

Utah
Division of Mental Health
Department of Human Services
120 N. 200 W., 4th Fl.
Salt Lake City, UT 84103
801-538-4270

Vermont
Mental Health & Retardation
Agency of Human Services
103 S. Main St.
Waterbury, VT 05671
802-241-2600

Virginia
Department of Mental Health,
  Retardation & Substance Abuse
  Services
109 Governor St.
Richmond, VA 23219
804-786-3921

Washington
Health & Rehabilitative Services
Department of Social & Health Services
P.O. Box 45060
Olympia, WA 98504
206-753-3327

West Virginia
Department of Health & Human Services
State Capitol Complex
Bldg. 6, Rm. B-617
Charleston, WV 25305
304-558-0684

Wyoming
Department of Health
117 Hathaway Building
Cheyenne, WY 82002
307-777-7656

Source: *State Administrative Officials Classified by Function 1993-1994*, The Council of State Governments, Lexington, KY, 1993.

CLUBHOUSES IN THE UNITED STATES AND CANADA

Alaska
Quyana Clubhouse
670 W. Fireweed Lane
Anchorage, AK 99503
907-265-4912

Arizona
East Valley Clubhouse
1310 W. University Dr.
Mesa, AZ 85201
602-835-0343

Our Place Clubhouse
39 N. 6th Ave.
Tucson, AZ 85701
602-884-5553

South Valley Clubhouse
1150 E. Washington
Phoenix, AZ 85006
602-257-4242

West Valley Clubhouse
5017 N. 35th Ave.
Phoenix, AZ 85017
602-973-1060

Arkansas
The N.E.W. Center
P.O. Box 2887
Fort Smith, AR 72913
501-452-9490

Rebuilders Club
1800 N. Maple St.
P.O. Box 9032
N. Little Rock, AR 72119
501-753-9583

Springhouse
P.O. Box 1340
Springdale, AR 72765
501-751-0066

California
Bayview Clubhouse
259 Hyde St.
San Francisco, CA 94102
415-928-6500

Hedco House
590 B St.
Hayward, CA 94546
510-247-8237

Towne House Creative Living Center
629 Oakland Ave.
Oakland, CA 94611
510-658-9480

Colorado
Chinook Clubhouse
1441 Broadway
Boulder, CO 80302
303-440-4842

Frontier House
1103 Fifth St.
Greeley, CO 80631
303-352-1095

Summit Center
10000 W. 21st Ave.
Lakewood, CO 80215
303-237-3733

Connecticut
Barrett House
235 White St.
Danbury, CT 06810
203-794-0819

Bridge House
880 Fairfield Ave.
Bridgeport, CT 06605
203-335-5339

Laurel House
6 Washington Ct.
Stamford, CT 06902
203-324-1816

Prime Time
41 E. Main St.
Torrington, CT 06790
203-482-3636

District of Columbia
Green Door
1623 16th St. NW
Washington, DC 20009
202-462-4092

Florida
Cope
P.O. Box 607
Dufuniek Springs, FL 32433
904-892-8035

Focus House
1585 NE 123rd St.
North Miami, FL 33161
305-895-4800

Georgia
Genesis
4540 Glenwood Rd.
Decatur, GA 30032
404-289-7701

Rainbow House
141 W. Solomon St.
Griffin, GA 30223
404-229-3090

Sunrise House
1828 Floyd Rd.
Columbus, GA 31909
706-568-0431

Hawaii
The Clubhouse
818 Sheridan St., #201
Honolulu, HI 96814
808-942-7494

Friendship House
P.O. Box 780
Kapaa, HI 96746
808-822-3244

Hale Pue Ilima
94-299 Farrington Hwy.
Waipahu, HI 96797
808-677-3158

Idaho
Confluence Clubhouse
1002 Idaho St.
Lewiston, ID 83501
208-746-1519

Harmabee Club
420 S. Main St.
Twin Falls, ID 83301
208-736-2114

Illinois
Independence Center
2025 Washington St.
Waukegan, IL 60085
708-360-1020

Indiana
New Hope Club
P.O. Box 817
Kendellville, IN 46755
219-347-4400

Iowa
New Horizons
915 Main St.
Adelk, IA 50003
515-993-3384

The Station
729 Pearl St.
Grinnell, IA 50112
515-236-5325

Rainbow Center
305 15th St.
Des Moines, IA 50309
515-243-6929

Kansas
Breakthrough Club
1005 E. 2nd
Wichita, KS 67214
316-269-2402

Grace House
1620 Janes
Winfield, KS 67156
316-221-3946

Louisiana
Audubon Friendship Club
830 Audubon St.
New Orleans, LA 70118
504-865-8770

Eastbank Friendship Club
3624 Florida St.
Kenner, LA 70062
504-464-7948

Westbank Friendship Club
2051 Eighth St.
Harvey, LA 70058
504-368-1944

Maryland
Omni House
P.O. Box 1270
Glen Burnie, MD 21060
410-768-6777

Way Station, Inc.
P.O. Box 3826
Frederick, MD 21705
301-694-0070

Massachusetts
There are over 20 clubhouses in MA, so I
will list the first six.

Atlantic House
338 Washington St.
Quincy, MA 02169
617-770-9660

Baybridge
209 Main St.
Hyannis, MA 02601
508-778-4234

Casa Primavera
114 Stoughton St.
Dorchester, MA 02125
617-825-3993

Center Club
31 Bowker St.
Boston, MA 02114
617-723-6300

Corner Clubhouse
P.O. Box 2037
247 Maple St.
Attleboro, MA 02703
508-226-5604

Crossroads at the Larches
11 Williams St.
Hopedale, MA 01747
508-473-4715

Michigan
There are numerous clubhouses in MI. I
will list the first six.

Bayside Lodge
3545 Bay Rd., Suite 7
Saginaw, MI 48603
517-799-1266

Crossroads Club
27041 Schoenherr Rd.
Warren, MI 48093
313-759-9100

Dreams Unlimited
13200 Oak Park Blvd.
Oak Park, MI 48237
810-547-7712

Fisher Center
2640 W. Vernor
Detroit, MI 48216
313-961-0360

Full Circle Community Center
102 N. Hamilton St.
Ypsilanti, MI 48198
314-485-2020

Genesis House
120 Grove St.
Battle Creek, MI 49017
616-966-1885

Minnesota
Vail Place
1412 W. 36th St.
Minneapolis, MN 55444
612-824-8061

Vail Place
15 9th Ave. South
Hopkins, MN 55343
612-938-9622

Mississippi
Friendship Clubhouse
P.O. Box 1505
Greenwood, MS 38930
601-455-3365

Pinnacle Clubhouse
2214 4th St.
Meridian, MS 39301
601-693-5051

Missouri
Independence Center
4380 W. Pine Blvd.
St. Louis, MO 63108
314-533-6511

Independence Center
9525 Midland Ave.
Overland, MO 653114
314-427-5597

Montana
Montana House
422 N. Last Chance Gulch
Helena, MT 59601
406-443-0794

Nebraska
Adams Street Center
3830 Adams St.
Lincoln, NE 68504
402-441-8150

Cirrus House
1509 First Ave.
Scottsbluff, NE 69361
308-635-1488

Frontier House
P.O. Box 1209
N. Platte, NE 69103
308-532-4730

Ivy House
4102 South 13th St.
Omaha, NE 68107
402-734-1614

Liberty Centre
112 S. Birch
Norfolk, NE 68701
402-371-1205

Opportunity House
P.O. Box 2066
Hastings, NE 68902
402-463-7435

New Jersey
The Club
UMDNH-CMHC
195 New St.
New Brunswick, NJ 08901
908-235-6900

Harbor House
703 Main St.
Paterson, NJ 07503
201-977-2156

Nevada
Arville House
1501 S. Arville
Las Vegas, NV 89102
702-259-4646

New York
New York has many clubhouses. Here
are six on the list.

Adirondack House
RD 1, Box 1012
Westport, NY 12993
518-962-8231

Beacon of Hope Clubhouse
512 Southern Blvd.
Bronx, NY 10455
718-993-1078

Bridges
212 Williams St.
Watertown, NY 13601
315-788-8092

The Chelton Loft
212 West 35th St., 4th Fl.
New York, NY 10001
212-290-2300

Clubhouse of Suffolk
P.O. Box 373
939 Johnson Ave.
Ronkonkoma, NY 11779
516-471-7242

Fountain House
425 W. 47th St.
New York, NY 10036
212-582-0340

North Carolina
Adventure House
924 N. Lafayette St.
Shelby, NC 28150
704-482-3370

Club Nova
103 D W. Main St.
Carrboro, NC 27510
919-968-6682

Magnolia House
429 W. Main St.
Forest City, NC 28043
704-248-2164

Ocean House
20 N. 4th St.
Wilmington, NC 28401
910-251-6590

Piedmont Pioneer House
910 Roberts Dr.
Gastonia, NC 28054
704-866-8751

River Club
1210 Old Cherry Pt. Rd.
New Bern, NC 28560
919-633-6431

North Dakota
Harmony Center
212 E. Central
Minot, ND 58701
701-852-3263

Ohio
Hill House
11101 Magnolia Dr.
Cleveland, OH 44106
216-721-3030

Pathway
1203 E. Broad St.
Columbus, OH 43205
614-251-2380

Oklahoma
Achievement House
4400 N. Lincoln St., Suite 100
Oklahoma City, OK 73105
405-424-7744

Crossroads
1812 E. 15th St.
Tulsa, OK 74104
918-749-2141

Pennsylvania
Chestnut Place Clubhouse
4042 Chestnut St.
Philadelphia, PA 19104
215-596-8200

Liberty House
12211 South 15th St.
Philadelphia, PA 19146
215-462-2030

Open Door Clubhouse
Collins and Cumberland St.
Philadelphia, PA 19125
215-427-5763

Welcome House
7700 Winchester Pike
Upper Darby, PA 19082
610-446-1485

Wellspring Clubhouse
915 Lawn Ave.
Sellersville, PA 18960
215-257-4760

Rhode Island
Hillsgrove House
70 Minnesota Ave.
Warwick, RI 02888
401-732-0970

Phoenix I
26 Spring St.
Newport, RI 02840
401-846-3135

South Carolina
New Day Clubhouse
P.O. Box 5396
189 S. Converse St.
Spartanburg, SC 29304
803-582-5431

South Dakota
5th St. Clubhouse
100 E. 5th St.
Sioux Falls, SD 57102
605-336-4503

Tennessee
Aim Center
1903 McCallie Ave.
Chattanooga, TN 37404
615-624-4800

Park Center
801 12th Ave. South
Nashville, TN 37203
615-242-3576

Texas
Independence House
334 Centre St.
Dallas, TX 75208
214-941-6054

Utah
Alliance House
1724 S. Main St.
Salt Lake City, UT 84115
801-486-5012

The Clubhouse
P.O. Box 553
Brigham City, UT 84302
801-723-3176

Davis Place
836 S. State St.
Clearfield, UT 84015
801-774-6580

Excel House
1079 E. Center St.
Provo, UT 84606
801-375-8308

Independence House
960 N. Dixie Downs Rd.
St. George, UT 84770
801-628-0612

Interact
198 E. Center St.
Moab, UT 84532
801-259-6131

Vermont
Carriage House
135 Granger St.
Rutland, VT 05701
802-775-7196

Evergreen House
24 Washington St.
Middlebury, VT 05756
802-388-3468

Mountain House
103 Burgess Rd.
Bennington, VT 05201
802-447-2166

Westview House
50 South Willard St.
Burlington, VT 05401
802-658-3323

Virginia
There are many clubhouses. Six are
listed here.

Beach House
3143 Magic Hollow Rd.
Virginia Beach, VA 23456
804-430-0368

Blueridge House
310 Avon St., Suite 10
Charlottesville, VA 22901
804-972-1825

Clarendon House
3141 N. 10th St.
Arlington, VA 22201
703-358-5236

Coastal Clubhouse
216 Great Bridge Blvd.
Chesapeake, VA 23320
804-547-0097

Highlands House
Route 10, Box 450
Abingdon, VA 24210
703-628-8513

Hospitality Center
5623 Tidewater Dr.
Norfolk, VA 23509
804-441-5310

Washington
Cascase Club
P.O. Box 1337
Vancouver, WA 98666
206-695-0257

Cowlitz River Club
537 14th Ave.
Longview, WA 98632
206-423-4243

Emerald House
1729 17th Ave.
Seattle, WA 98122
206-324-9362

Evergreen Club
2102 Sprague Ave., East
Spokane, WA 99202
509-458-7454

Freedom House
19630 76th Ave., West
Lynnwood, WA 98026
206-775-8583

Harvest House
338 NE Maple St.
Pullman, WA 99163
509-334-6873

Wisconsin
Grand Avenue Club
734 N. 4th St.
Milwaukee, WI 53203
414-276-6474

Yahara House
802 E. Gorham St.
Madison, WI 53703
608-257-7757

Canada
This is a partial list.

Cambridge Clubhouse
117 Main St.
Cambridge, Ontario
CANADA N1R 1W1
519-740-7766

Causeway
20 Graham Ave.
Ottawa, Ontario
CANADA K1S0B7
613-230-9557

Coast Foundation Clubhouse
295 East 11th Ave.
Vancouver, B.C.
CANADA V5T 2C5
604-876-6345

Connections Clubhouse
2494 Robie St.
Halifax, Canada B3K 4N1
902-496-2696

Notre Dame Place
67 Duke St.
Summerside, Prince Edward Island
CANADA C1N 3R9
902-436-7399

Pathways Clubhouse
Unite 160-5811
Cedarbridge Way
Richmond, B.C.
CANADA V6X 2A8
604-276-8834

Source Club
6239 Walnut St.
Powell River, B.C.
CANADA V8A 4K4
604-483-3989

Source: This information was provided by the International Center for Clubhouse Development at Fountain House, Inc. in New York.

BIBLIOGRAPHY

Ambert, Anne-Marie, Ph.D., *The Effect of Children on Parents* (New York: The Haworth Press, 1992).

American Academy of Family Physicians, "Review of Suicide in Patients with Major Depression," *American Family Physician,* Oct. 1994, v. 50, n. 5, p. 1102(2).

Andrews, Howard; Barker, Joan; Pittman, John; Mars, Larry; Struening, Elmer; and LaRocca, Nicholas, "National Trends in Vocational Rehabilitation: A Comparison of Individuals with Physical Disabilities and Individuals with Psychiatric Disabilities," *The Journal of Rehabilitation*, Jan.-March 1992, v. 58, n. 1, p.7(1).

Anthony, William A. and Jansen, Mary A., "Predicting the Vocational Capacity of the Chronically Mentally Ill," *American Psychologist*, May 1984, v. 39, n. 5, pp. 537-544.

Anthony, William and Blanch, Andrea, "Supported Employment for Persons Who Are Psychiatrically Disabled: An Historical and Conceptual Perspective," *Psychosocial Rehabilitation Journal*, Oct. 1987, v. XI, n. 2, pp. 5-22.

Atkinson, Jacqueline M., Ph.D., *Schizophrenia at Home: A Guide to Helping the Family* (New York: New York University Press).

The Best of the AMI/FAMI Reporter, Sept./Oct. 1992, v. 12-7A.

Block, Bruce and Pristach, Cynthia A., "Diagnosis and Management of the Paranoid Patient," *American Family Physician*, June 1992, v. 45, n. 6, p. 2634 (7).

Bordwin, Milton, "ADA: The Americans With and Without Disabilities Act," *Management Review*, May 1995, v. 84, n. 5, p. 53(4).

Brakel, Samuel Jan, J.D., and Davis, John M., M.D., "Taking Harms Seriously: Involuntary Mental Patients and the Right to Refuse Treatment," *Indiana Law Review*, 1991, v. 25, p. 429-473.

Cook, Judith A., "Who 'Mothers' the Chronically Mentally Ill?", *Family Relations*, Jan. 1988, v. 37, p. 42(7).

Dowling, Colette, *You Mean I Don't Have to Feel This Way? New Help for Depression, Anxiety and Addiction* (New York: Charles Scribner's Sons, 1991).

Drake, Robert E., M.D., Ph.D., "Substance Abuse and Mental Illness: Recent Research," *NAMI Advocate,* Jan./Feb. 1995, v. 16, n. 4, p. 5(2).

Dumont, Matthew, "Deep in the Heart of Chelsea," *Mother Jones*, March-April 1994, v. 19, n. 2, p. 60(5).

Fadden, Grainne; Bebbington, Paul; and Kuipers, Liz, "The Burden of Care; The Impact of Functional Psychiatric Illness on the Patient's Family," *British Journal of Psychiatry*, 1987, v. 150, pp. 285-292.

Fadden, Grainne; Bebbington, Paul; and Kuipers, Liz, "Caring and Its Burdens: A Study of the Spouses of Depressed Patients," *British Journal of Psychiatry*, 1987, v. 151, pp. 660-667.

Fink, Paul Jay, M.D., and Tasman, Allan, M.D., Eds. (Washington, DC: American Psychiatric Press, 1992).

Gilhooly, Mary L. M., "The Impact of Care-Giving on Care-Givers: Factors Associated with the Psychological Well-Being of People Supporting a Dementing Relative in the Community," *British Journal of Medical Psychology*, 1984, v. 57, pp. 35-44.

Gorman, Christine, "Suicide Check: Advances in Biopsychiatry May Lead to Lab Tests for Self-Destructive Behavior and Other Mental Disorders," *Time*, Nov. 28, 1994, v. 144, n. 22, p. 65(2).

Gottesman, Irving I., *Schizophrenia Genesis: The Origins of Madness* (New York: W.H. Freeman and Company, 1991).

Grad, Jacqueline, Ph.D., and Sainsbury, Peter, M.D., D.P.M., "Mental Illness and the Family," *The Lancet*, March 9, 1963, pp. 544-547.

Gubman, Gayle D. and Tessler, Richard C., "The Impact of Mental Illness on Families: Concepts and Priorities," *Journal of Family Issues*, June 1987, v. 8, No. 2, pp. 226-245.

Hatfield, Agnes B. and Lefley, Harriet P., *Families of the Mentally Ill* (New York: The Guilford Press, 1987).

Herman, Nancy, "Return to Sender: Reintegrative Stigma-Management Strategies of Ex-Psychiatric Patients," *Journal of Contemporary Ethnography*, October 1993, v. 22, n. 3, pp. 295-330.

Hinrichsen, Gregory A., Ph.D., and Niederehe, George, Ph.D., "Dementia Management Strategies and Adjustment of Family Members of Older Patients," *The Gerontologist*, 1994, v. 34, n. 1, pp. 95-102.

Isaac, Rael Jean, *Madness in the Streets: How Psychiatry and the Law Abandoned the Mentally Ill* (New York: The Free Press, 1990).

Isaac, Rael Jean and Brakel, Samuel Jan, "Subverting Good Intentions: A Brief History of Mental Health Law 'Reform'," *Cornell Journal of Law and Public Policy*, Fall 1992, v. 2, n. 1, pp. 89-119.

Jaffe, D. J., "How to Force the System to Give You or Your Relative Better Care," undated paper provided by the author in 1995.

Johnson, Ann Braden, *Out of Bedlam: The Truth About Deinstitutionalization* (New York: Basic Books, 1990).

Kaihla, Paul, "A Mother's Tragic Tale," *Maclean's*, March 6, 1995, v. 108, n. 10, p. 56(3).

Kalichman, Seth C.; Kelly, Jeffrey A.; Johnson, Jennifer R.; Bulto, Marita, "Factors Associated with Risk for HIV Infection Among Chronic Mentally Ill Adults," *American Journal of Orthopsychiatry*, Feb. 1994, v. 151, n. 2, p. 221(7).

Kaplan, Robert J., J.D., "Outpatient Commitment Info," paper published by the National Alliance for the Mentally Ill, Arlington, Virginia, 1995.

Katschnig, Heinz and Konieczna, Teresa, "What Works in Work with Relatives? A Hypothesis," *British Journal of Psychiatry*, 1989, v. 155 (supp. 5), pp. 144-150.

Keefe, S. E., Richard, and Harvey, Philip D., *Understanding Schizophrenia: A Guide to the New Research on Causes and Treatment* (New York: The Free Press, 1994).

Lafond, Virginia, *Grieving Mental Illness: A Guide for Patients and Their Caregivers* (Toronto, Canada: University of Toronto Press, 1994).

Lefley, Harriet P., Ph.D., and Johnson, Dale L., Ph.D., Eds., *Families as Allies in Treatment of the Mentally Ill: New Directions for Mental Health Professionals* (Washington, DC: American Psychiatric Press, 1990).

Link, Bruce, G.; Mirotznik, Jerrold; and Cullen, Francis T., "The Effectiveness of Stigma Coping Orientations: Can Negative Consequences of Mental Illness Labeling Be Avoided?" *Journal of Health and Social Behavior*, Sept. 1991, v. 32, pp. 302-320.

Mansheim, Paul A., M.D., "Working with Families on an Inpatient Psychiatric Unit for Children: Hospital Staff Members Are Family Therapists, Too," *Contemporary Family Therapy*, Winter 1989, v. 11, no. 4, pp. 267-275.

Marrone, Joe and Gold, Martine, "Supported Employment for People with Mental Illness: Myths and Facts," *The Journal of Rehabilitation*, Oct.-Dec. 1994, v. 60, n. 4, p. 38(10).

Marsh, Diane T., *Families and Mental Illness: New Directions in Professional Practice* (New York: Praeger, 1992).

McElroy, Evelyn, Ph.D., Ed., *Children and Adolescents with Mental Illness: A Parent's Guide* (Kensington, Maryland: Woodbine House, 1988).

Mellins, Claude A.; Blum, Mindy J.; Boyd-Davis, Sandra L.; Gatz, Margaret, "Family Network Perspectives on Caregiving," *Generations*, Winter-Spring 1993, v. 17, n. 1, p. 21(4).

Mermier, Martha Brinton, *Coping with Severe Mental Illness: Families Speak Out* (Lewiston, NY: The Edwin Mellen Press, 1993).

Moscovine, Ira; Lurie, Nicole; Christianson, Jon; Finch, Michael; Popkin, Michael; Akhtar, Muhammad R., "Access and Use of Health Services by Chronically Mentally Ill Medicaid Beneficiaries," *Health Care Financing Review*, Summer 1993, v. 14, n. 4, p. 75(13).

Mueser, Kim T., Ph.D. and Gingerich, Susan, M.S.W., *Coping with Schizophrenia: A Guide for Families* (Oakland, CA: New Harbinger Publications, Inc., 1994).

Mulligan, Kate, "Help for Families with Mentally Ill Children," *AARP Bulletin*, February 1995, v. 36, n. 2, p. 12.

Namyslowska, Irena, "Social and Emotional Adaptation of the Families of Schizophrenic Patients," *Family Systems Medicine*, Winter 1986, v. 4, n. 4, 1986, pp. 398-407.

Noll, Richard, M.A., *The Encyclopedia of Schizophrenia and the Psychotic Disorders* (New York: Facts on File, Inc., 1992).

Northouse, Laurel Lindhout, R.N., "Who Supports the Support System?" *Journal of Psychosocial Nursing and Mental Health Services*, May 1980, pp. 11-15.

Perring, Christina; Twigg, Julia; and Atkin, Karl, *Families Caring for People Diagnosed as Mentally Ill: The Literature Re-Examined* (London, England: HMSO Social Policy Research Unit, 1992).

Peschel, Enid; Peschel, Richard; Howe, Carol W.; Howe, James W., Eds., *Neurobiological Disorders in Children and Adolescents* (San Francisco: Jossey-Bass, 1992).

Pittman, Frank, III, "A Buyer's Guide to Psychotherapy," *Psychology Today*, Jan.-Feb. 1994, v. 27, n. 1, p. 50(10).

Rakel, Robert E., "Don't Underestimate Clues That Signal Severe Depression," *Consultant*, Sept. 1989, v. 29, n. 9, p. 109(6).

Reynolds, Maynard C., "Child Disabilities: Who's In, Who's Out," *Journal of School Health*, Aug. 1994, v. 64, n. 6, p. 238(4).

Richardson, Brenda Lane, "Talking to Walls," *Essence*, July 1994, v. 25, n. 3, p. 58(6).

Roesch, Roberta, *The Encyclopedia of Depression* (New York: Facts on File, Inc., 1991).

Roha, Ronaleen R. and Richmond, Suzan, "Financial Planning When Your Child Is Disabled," *Changing Times*, Dec. 1988, v. 42, n. 12, p. 79(4).

Russell, L. Mark, J.D.; Grant, Arnold E., J.D.; Joseph, Suzanne M., C.F.P; and Fee, Richard W., M.ED, M.A., *Planning for the Future* (Evanston, IL: American Publishing Company, 1994).

Ryde-Brandt, Brita, "Anxiety and Depression in Mothers of Children with Psychotic Disorders and Mental Retardation," *British Journal of Psychiatry*, 1990, v. 156, p. 118(4).

Sileo, Chi Chi, "Under Fire, Therapy Faces a Backlash," *Insight on the News*, Aug. 29, 1994, v. 10, no. 35, p. 6(6).

Sommers, Ira, D.S.W., "The Influence of Environmental Factors on the Community Adjustment of the Mentally Ill," *The Journal of Nervous and Mental Disease*, 1988, v. 176, n. 4, pp. 221-226.

Terkelsen, Kenneth G., M.D., "Schizophrenia and the Family: II. Adverse Effects of Family Therapy," *Family Process,* June 1983, v. 22, pp. 191-200.

Thompson, Jr., Edward H. and Doll, William, "The Burden of Families Coping with the Mentally Ill: An Invisible Crisis," *Family Relations*, July 1982, v. 31, pp. 379-388.

Torrey, E. Fuller, M.D., *Surviving Schizophrenia: A Manual for Families, Consumers and Providers* (New York: Harper Perennial, 1995).

U.S. Social Security Administration, "When You Get SSI: What You Need to Know," SSA Publication No. 05-11011, June 1994.

U.S. Social Security Administration, "A Guide to SSI for Groups and Organizations," SSA Publication No. 05-11015, March 1995.

INDEX

ABOUT THE AUTHOR

Christine Adamec was born in Malden, Massachusetts. A "military brat," she had attended twelve schools by the time she graduated from high school, including one in Izmir, Turkey. She received her Bachelor's degree in psychology from the University of New Hampshire and her Master's in Business Administration from New Hampshire College.

After college graduation, Ms. Adamec received her commission as an Air Force officer and served on active duty. She was awarded the Air Force Commendation Medal for her service. Subsequently an Air Force Reservist, Ms. Adamec retired from the Air Force Reserve with the rank of major.

Ms. Adamec has been a professional writer since 1981, and has written hundreds of magazine features for such diverse publications as *McCall's, Employee Relations & Human Resources Bulletin, 80 Micro, Executive Female,* and *Expo Magazine.* Ms. Adamec has also assisted many businesspeople, attorneys, and physicians by editing and writing articles, pamphlets, and books. The common denominator, says Adamec, is that everything she writes, no matter how brief or extensive, has the underlying goal of helping the reader in some way. Her self-help books include *There ARE Babies to Adopt* (updated for Kensington, 1996) and *Start and Run a Profitable Freelance Writing Business* (Self-Counsel Press, 1994).

She lives in Palm Bay, Florida, with her husband and their three children.